# Women
## FOR
# Peace

# Women
## FOR
# Peace

MARLENE TARG BRILL

WOMEN THEN, WOMEN NOW

FRANKLIN WATTS
A Division of Grolier Publishing
New York London Hong Kong Sydney
Danbury, Connecticut

*For Alison, Rich, Dena, and Harry, who have the courage to fight for a more peaceful world.*

Interior Design by Molly Heron
Photographs ©: AP/Wide World Photos: 115; Archive Photos: 33, 53; Brown Brothers: 63, 77; Corbis-Bettmann: 18, 20, 57; Culver Pictures: 69; The Library of Congress: 48; The New York Historical Society: 40; The Peace Museum: 134 (Timothy D. Lace); Reuters/Corbis-Bettmann: 10; Schoharie Museum of the Iroquois Indian: 27; Sophia Smith Collection, Smith College, Northampton, MA: 45, 66; Swarthmore College Peace Collection: 80, 105, 119; UPI/Corbis-Bettmann: 83, 88, 91, 101, 106, 117, 128, 137, 140.

Library of Congress Cataloging-in-Publication Data
    Brill, Marlene Targ.
      Women for peace / Marlene Targ Brill.
         p.  cm. — (Women then, women now)
      Includes bibliographical references and index.
      ISBN 0-531-11328-0
      1. Women and peace. 2. Women and peace—United States. I. Title. II. Series: Women then—women now.
      JX1965.B74 1997
      327.1'72'082—cd20
      96-28945                      CIP

# Contents

# Peace as a Women's Issue

# 1

**D**r. Anna Howard Shaw rose to speak before the first Woman's Peace Party convention on January 10, 1915. A grave hush settled over the audience as Shaw began her passionate plea. She urged women from every walk of life to protest the approaching war. Then she scolded the men who challenged a woman's right to fight for peace. "Looking into his [a soldier's] dead face someone asks a woman, what does a woman know about war? . . . [I]n the face of a crime like that," Shaw asks firmly, "what does a man know about war?"[1]

For centuries, societies have disregarded women's opinions of war and peace. Traditional histories offer a view of the world through men's eyes. Records focus almost entirely on men's achievements, lives, and wars. Little has been written about peace, and even less appears about women's role in creating peaceful communities.

Yet more than half of the antislavery activists were women. And women ran the only major organized peace group to oppose U.S. participation in World War I, the

Woman's Peace Party (later known as the Women's International League for Peace and Freedom). Today, women conduct revolutionary campaigns against nuclear arms, domestic violence, and many other social, political, and environmental issues. Exploring women's role in history reveals their rich legacy as active change makers and dynamic peace builders.

## A HISTORY OF VIOLENCE

Women's peaceful efforts seem more important when we understand the extent of violence that invades our lives. Scholars document 3,357 wars in the years between 1496 B.C. and A.D. 1941—almost one war each year. Include the armed skirmishes that flare and die quickly, and the number soars higher. More than 278 wars and 2,700 major conflicts occurred between Columbus's 1492 landing in North America and 1941.[2] That's almost seven clashes every year. Since World War II, the violence has spread unchecked to newly independent nations. During the 1990s, 34 armed conflicts raged around the world in a single 12-month period.[3]

After each campaign everything changes for the countries involved. Even in the nations that triumph, war takes a toll on lives, property, and the environment. Old beliefs and goals assume different meanings after war. Nations and their citizens are never the same again.

The United States has withstood its share of war, beginning with the country's violent birth. First, colonists forced Native Americans off their land. Then they battled their English king in the Revolutionary War (1775–83), which cost the 13 colonies $101.1 million and 25,324 American lives.[4] More conflicts followed as settlers moved farther west. To many colonists, the rewards of aggression were worth the losses. They gained freedom from England and a new expanding nation.

Since its violent beginning, the United States has launched a constant stream of military battles. Nine major wars and more than 200 armed invasions have occurred since 1776.[5] From 1977 to 1993, the United States sent armed troops to carry out 32 invasions abroad.[6] A nation born of violence has created one of the most powerful militaries in the world.

Has the world ever achieved lasting peace? Sadly, not for very long. We live in a world where too many people fight. Even when a major conflict ends, smaller clashes—within nations or neighborhoods—persist around the globe. Soldiers cross borders, governments harass citizens, and partners abuse each other and their children.

Whenever hostilities erupt, however, there are people who refuse to accept violence as the only way to settle differences. Every battle unites individuals or groups that strongly oppose war. And as long as protest has existed, women's voices have led special calls for peace.

Government leaders believe that a strong military protects U.S. citizens from dangerous nations. The military's long arms reach to acquire new land or silence rebellions in countries worthy of U.S. support. Most Americans have agreed with government views on this military policy. But some women, as well as men, have always disapproved of any violence. They have joined peace organizations and have written and lectured as individuals to end war and the causes of violence.

Today, women still seek a world without tyranny, poverty, and injustice—a world where people matter. Many press for better living and working conditions, reproductive choice, quality childcare, an end to abuse at home, and a safer, healthier environment.

## WOMEN AND MEN AS PEACEMAKERS

Do such interests mean women are more peaceful and men more warlike? Not necessarily. Traditionally, both men and women have viewed women as the peace-loving, gentler sex. Yet, there have been repeated examples of men who oppose conflict and women who promote war in various ways.

BOSNIAN REFUGEES—GRANDMOTHER, MOTHER, AND CHILDREN—GAZE OUT A WINDOW AT A REFUGEE CENTER. WOMEN WORLDWIDE SEEK A WORLD WITHOUT TYRANNY, POVERTY, INEQUALITY, AND WAR.

Almost every nation has stories of women who proudly pushed their sons into battle. In the United States, women supported the Civil War by making and collecting supplies for military camps and by nursing soldiers. Wives ran farms and businesses so men could fight. During the twentieth century, women held government posts and took factory jobs to free men for battle during world wars I and II. Some women joined such groups as the Red Cross, which provided aid wherever fighting occurred.

In every major war, women have followed men into combat. Betsy Sullivan, known as the mother to the First Tennessee Regiment, nursed her husband and his company of soldiers during the Civil War. One man wrote later, "not one single man in the entire regiment would have hesitated to spill the last drop of blood for 'Mother Sullivan.' "[7]

There are many stories of women who fought alongside men as soldiers. Of these, Deborah Sampson is the most celebrated. In October 1778 Sampson left her family in Plymouth, Massachusetts, dressed as a man and headed for battle. Soldiers were not given physical exams back then, so Sampson easily enlisted in the Continental army as Robert Shirtliffe. Sampson fought bravely in a number of battles until a bullet lodged in her shoulder. Sampson's first reaction was a "sickening terror . . . that her sex would be discovered."[8] General George Washington honorably discharged Sampson, never revealing her secret.

Women have also proven forceful as government leaders. Between 1969 and 1974, Israeli prime minister Golda Meir often chose battle to defend her country's borders. In 1982, Margaret Thatcher sent British troops to recapture the Falkland Islands, a British colony that had been occupied by Argentina's army, rather than negotiate a settlement over ownership of the islands. Both women challenge traditional assumptions about women's views on violence.

Still, many societies insist on dividing males and females into assigned roles. The myth of men going off to war while women nurture lingers. Even though both sexes have the capacity for aggression and resolving conflict, scientists continue to question whether males are less peaceful.

Is the difference inborn or does society create males who are more suitable for combat? Some research indicates that beyond the obvious anatomy, males and females *are* born different. On the average women have 50 percent less upper-body strength than men. Many military experts contend that this makes men better suited as soldiers.

Studies with scanners that record brain activity point to differences in how men and women process information.

Researchers claim that variations may be due to the way the brain uses the male hormone testosterone and female hormone estrogen. Different levels of both hormones are found in males and females. The combination of these hormones in the brain affects aggressive behavior.

When female baby rats receive testosterone, they fight more as adults. Likewise, male rats with added female hormone tend to show fewer aggressive behaviors. Although recent studies with humans cloud the picture of which hormone causes people to fight, researchers agree that there are differences in how hormones work in males and females.[9]

Many critics believe that differences between how men and women view violence really come from the world we live in. Quaker peace activist Elise Hanson Boulding agrees:

> *I don't think women are naturally more peaceful than men. They have to learn to be peaceful, just like men do: but women are in situations where they develop their peaceable capabilities, such as child rearing. . . . Men who are removed from that process of human growth don't get the same things to cultivate that peaceable nature.*[10]

Society continues to push traditional roles on boys and girls. For males there is the connection between manliness and violence. Communities hold holiday events surrounding Memorial Day and Veterans Day and build statues of soldiers in parks. Children celebrate war and study male warriors in school. Few teachers talk about those women who resist war. Instead, many history books, newspapers, television, and movies glorify male violence.

At home, many parents handle male and female babies differently. Boys get tossed into the air more frequently; girls are cradled or cuddled in the arms. Parents dress boys in bold primary colors and buy them toys that promote competition and war making. By the time they become adults, many males are unable to prove they are men unless they are violent or soldiers.

A 1915 poster titled "Why We Oppose Votes for Men" jokes about the way society supports a man's need for aggression. The reasons quoted come from Alice Duer Miller, a woman's movement pioneer who wrote:

> *Men shouldn't vote: 1. Because men are too emotional to vote. Their conduct at baseball games and political conventions show this, while their innate tendency to appeal to force renders them particularly unfit for the task of government. 2. Because no really manly man wants to settle any question other than by fighting about it. 3. Because man's place is in the army. 4. Because men will lose their charm if they step out of their natural sphere and interest themselves in other matters than feats of arms, uniforms, and drums. 5. Because, if men should adopt peaceable methods, women will no longer look up to them.*[11]

Unlike men, most women have been excluded from aggressive, competitive, and combative pursuits for centuries. Parents tend to dress female babies in soft pastel colors, even down to the throwaway diapers. They fill baby girls' cribs with stuffed animals and dolls. Young girls learn to be more peaceful and nurturing through activities that mold their actions that way. Many learn to accept unmet needs just as some boys learn to destroy others to meet goals.

To combat child-rearing differences, critics encourage parents to treat their children fairly—as individuals rather than boys or girls. Many adults go out of their way to give boys and girls opportunities that help them be the best people they can be. They offer nonviolent toys and action games to children of both sexes. Still, several studies over the past 20 years reveal a small but significant difference remaining in how females and males view peace, war, and military spending. Twenty percent more women than men in the United States vote for more peaceful government actions.

Similarly, a 1991 *Scholastic Update* poll of 110,000 teenagers found variations in how boys and girls responded to U.S. actions after Iraq invaded Kuwait. At the time, U.S. armed forces were sent to the Persian Gulf region. The major reason for involvement was to protect U.S. oil interests in Kuwait and Saudi Arabia. Girls and boys were equally angry about sending troops into the Middle East; although significantly more girls (70.8 percent) than boys (33.7 percent) viewed the prospect of war as scary.

When asked if military force was the right way to go, more boys (69 percent) than girls (48.3 percent) agreed. More boys (40.3 percent) than girls (26.4 percent) felt proud and excited about the move, and twice as many girls (34.5 percent) as boys (17.6 percent) expressed that no reason was good enough to go to war.[12]

Do these studies confirm that girls and women are really more peaceful? No one can say for sure. What we do know is that in every historical era women have taken action in the name of peace, equality, and justice. They believed the men in power made dangerous decisions that threatened life and property.

Women are not the sole keepers of peace, but they play—and will continue to play—a significant role as people who bring about and maintain world harmony. Peace will always be a woman's issue.

# ANCIENT HERSTORY

# 2

*The Attic woman is no slave. . . . War shall be a care to women!*

—from Aristophanes's play *Lysistrata*[1]

The roots of women's peacekeeping began thousands of years before America's founding. Between 10,000 B.C. and 6000 B.C., the first civilizations emerged along the fertile river valleys. As settlements developed into city-states, nomads and landlords battled over land and water rights. New empires prayed to goddesses for their unusual powers over war and peace. The primary peacemaking role of women was to create and nurture.

## GODDESSES AND PROPHETS

More than 5,000 years ago early Egyptians credited Isis, the goddess of wisdom, with founding their farming culture. Isis introduced wheat and discovered the healthful values of fruits and nuts. She developed a way to spin flax into linen. Her cleverness guided the weaving of linen into sails, giving Egyptians the first boats propelled by sails. Isis taught Egyptians to communicate by writing and gave them a whole new way to live.

Along the nearby Tigris River valley in modern Iraq, the Mesopotamians praised Ishtar, a goddess of love, fertility, and war. Ishtar awakened the dead and healed the sick. Her strength kept soldiers safe during battle. By about 2500 B.C., however, foreigners raided Mesopotamia. They crushed the armies and plundered the land. Hungry and defeated townspeople condemned Ishtar and the other goddesses for their severe losses. Thereafter, the people prayed to male warrior gods instead.

Wisdom helped many Semitic women of the Bible keep peace. The Old Testament tells how Abigail prevented David, a warrior and future king of Judah, from killing her husband Moan. David and his followers lived in the wilderness, where water and meat became scarce. So David sent his men in peace to ask the wealthy shepherd for food and drink. Greedy Moan refused to help and turned David's men away in anger. David's warrior response was, "Every man strap on his sword!"

One of Moan's servants sneaked away to tell Abigail. More reasonable than her husband, Abigail quickly rode to David with words of apology and donkeys weighted with drinks and foods. Fortunately, David agreed that bloodshed was unnecessary. He told Abigail, "Blessed be your good sense, and blessed be you, who have kept me today from bloodguilt and from avenging myself by my own hand!"[2]

While men improved the art of war, early women from many societies perfected the more peaceful, life-giving arts. Early Greeks credited their goddess Pallas Athena with inventing olives, the backbone of the country's economy. The Roman goddess Minerva provided the first homes of earth, stone, or mud. According to Chinese legend, Xilingshi, wife of the emperor Huangdi, earned the title Goddess of Silkworms for her discovery of silk in 2700 B.C. Four Chinese girls introduced silk preparation and weaving into Japan. The new industry became a source of great wealth and trade for both countries, and the grateful Japanese constructed a temple to honor the girls in the Setsu province.

Through these and countless other efforts, families and

communities had what they needed to stay more peaceful. But as communities progressed, so did the technology of weapons and warfare. Male strength encouraged heavier metal tools and machinery. As ancient villages and kingdoms expanded, men displaced women in areas of trade, agriculture, and some crafts. Male gods replaced female goddesses. Women's influence outside childbearing and homemaking declined. Nevertheless, women had their say in matters of war and peace. Men heard women's collective voices through music, dance, and rituals. Women used these methods to protest violence, much as they do today.[3]

One Egyptian woman, however, influenced an entire empire. *Hatshepsut* became pharaoh, or ruler, in about 1480 B.C. She rose to power at a time when male pharaohs sought to conquer weaker nations to acquire slave labor and when they built pyramid temples to honor themselves and the male sun god, Ra. By then, peaceful female goddesses, such as Isis, the goddess of wisdom, and Maat, the goddess of moral judgment, had faded in importance. Yet Hatshepsut managed to reverse the conflicts started by her warlike predecessors. During her 20-year reign, she sent peaceful trading parties to other countries, ruled with fairness, and brought harmony to the empire. Her main problems stemmed from being a woman and a widow. To assert control, Hatshepsut was forced to invent ancestry from a male god and wear a false beard.[4]

About 1,000 years later, Greek men governed the home and affairs of state much like their Egyptian neighbors. Any woman who disobeyed her husband or father often paid a terrible price. None suffered more, yet is more inspiring to peace seekers, than the title character in the play *Antigone*. Sophocles wrote this stirring tragedy in 442 B.C. In the play, Antigone—a woman who defied her fiancé's father, the king of Thebes—insists that women have the right and the duty to resist authority in the service of higher moral law.

Antigone sincerely believes that her brother died unjustly in battle. When she gives her brother a proper burial

THIS SCULPTURE DEPICTS HATSHEPSUT, QUEEN OF ANCIENT EGYPT.

against her father-in-law's wishes, the king buries Antigone alive for her bold action. Today, women peace seekers find strength in Antigone's courage, dignity, and perseverance.

The Peloponnesian War between Athens and Sparta (433 B.C.–404 B.C.) gave rise to new thinking about women's role in society. Greek philosopher Plato wrote, "in the administration of a State, neither a woman as a woman nor a man as a man has any special function, but the gifts of nature are equally diffused in both sexes. . . . And one woman has a turn for gymnastic and military exercises, while another is unwarlike and hates gymnastics."[5] Plato believed that everyone deserved equal opportunities. Therefore, women should receive the same education as men and be permitted a voice in government matters. Most Greeks found Plato's ideas outrageous, although the city of Athens was named after the battle goddess Athena, and many Spartan women proudly sent their sons to war.

Greek playwright Aristophanes reflected on what women could accomplish if given the chance. In his comic play *Lysistrata* (ca. 415 B.C.), Aristophanes brings together women characters from different city-states to protest war through common action, which was revolutionary in itself. The Greek women have endured 10 years of men's military blunders without saying a word. Lysistrata, the wife of an Athenian magistrate, declares that women suffered double pain from war—as wives who are deprived of their soldier husbands and as mothers who send sons to die.

Lysistrata urges the women to refuse lovemaking and all child care and household chores until their men end the war. Women protesters take over the government treasury building to prevent funds from being spent on the war. *Lysistrata* has several funny scenes with men holding screaming children and pleading with their wives to come home. The women's tactics to bring about an end to the war prove successful.

The earliest documented nonviolent demonstration by women was in 195 B.C. Roman law prohibited women

ATHENIAN PLAYWRIGHT ARISTOPHANES ILLUSTRATED THE
POTENTIAL POWER OF WOMEN IN HIS COMEDY *LYSISTRATA*.

from wearing purple and gold in public and riding in horse-drawn carriages within towns and cities. These were signs of authority reserved for powerful men only. Statesmen explained that the law was merely a way to discourage wastefulness by spoiled rich women, but women in Rome and the surrounding countryside disagreed, mobbing the streets to object. The law was repealed[6]

About 300 B.C., another peaceful protest defended a woman's right to practice medicine, which was forbidden under the laws of Athens. Despite the law, Agnodice dressed as a man and treated women in Athens. After her disguise was discovered, authorities jailed, tried, and banished Agnodice from the country. Crowds of Athenian women came to her defense. They swarmed the jail and threatened to end all lovemaking until Agnodice was set free. As in *Lysistrata*, women who organized nonviolent protest triumphed.

## RISE OF CHRISTIANITY

For the next 1,500 years, Christianity gained a foothold in Europe. Politics and religion blended as the Roman Catholic church increased its power. Early followers of Jesus Christ heeded his words, "Blessed are the peacemakers,"[7] and tried to stay out of war.

Then Saint Augustine (354–430) defended the right of good Christians to protect the faith. His ideas later gave cause for what was called the "just war." Between 1000 and 1400, a series of violent wars arose in the name of the church. In 1095 the Council of Clermont launched the first holy war, or Crusade, killing more than 800,000 people.

Women and men protested the violence. The church responded by sponsoring Peace of God and Truce of God campaigns. Women participated in the campaigns to:

*limit the days on which fighting could take place, and restrict those involved in conflict by exempting from assault and destruction clerics, monks, nuns, women,*

21

*pilgrims, merchants, peasants, visitors to councils,*
*churches, and their surrounding grounds, cemeteries*
*and cloisters, the lands of the clergy, shepherds and*
*their flocks, agricultural animals, wagons in the*
*fields and olive trees. Landlords and knights took*
*oaths agreeing to limit their sacking of villages and*
*each other.*[8]

Church leaders increasingly limited women's role in public issues. Nevertheless, individual women found ways to assert their independence against fierce church control. Peaceful protests for some women included dancing or washing clothes on Sundays and holy days, which was forbidden. Other women became "unmannerly in churches."[9] In medieval author Christine de Pisan's fable, *The Book of the City of Ladies,* three goddesses—Righteousness, Reason, and Justice—govern a peaceful city of only women. The author proclaims war to be foolish and wasteful. Pisan's Wise Princess character advises a Christian prince how to rule firmly yet justly.

In twelfth-century Belgium, groups of women called Beguines lived together and developed their own religious practices. Without benefit of men or the Roman Catholic church, the Beguines preached goodness and peace. Slowly, their way of living spread to women in France, Germany, and throughout Europe.

The Crusades, however, caused the church to tighten its control on laws, education, and private lives. In its eagerness to rule, the church sought to silence different religious views. Dominican monks held trials, or inquisitions, to judge whether individuals acted against church teachings. The idea that women could govern themselves independently and preach outside church teachings was unacceptable to the monks.

Beguine leaders faced torture and death for preaching peace in public and writing Bible translations and psalms. The Beguines died out after about 100 years. Some Beguine settlements reappeared in seventeenth-century Belgium. Today, only a few Beguine communities in Belgium and the Netherlands remain.

During the early sixteenth century, Martin Luther, a German professor of religion, successfully challenged church rituals and the supreme authority of the pope. Luther believed that true Christians answered to God and their country, in that order. For him, government had no place in religion. Luther found little use for church hierarchy and practices, such as confession. He called for the first major religious reform in Christianity.

Luther gained a large following of Protestant reformers. Protestants clashed with the Catholic church in a series of religious battles that ended with the Thirty Years' War (1618–48) in Germany. To stifle growing disagreement, the church responded with another Inquisition.

This time women who influenced their communities were branded as witches. Church leaders accused women of casting wicked spells, an offense impossible to prove or disprove. Midwives, healers, and any women who questioned the church's cruel treatment were targets of witch-hunts. Witch-hunts spread throughout Europe and to North American colonies. Between the middle of the fifteenth century and early eighteenth century, almost nine million people, mostly women, died for some opinion that threatened local religious leaders.

Despite the witch-hunts, Luther's spirit of change sparked lasting reform that resulted in other branches of Protestantism. Several peaceful religious sects formed. The Society of Friends from England, the Moravian Church from eastern Europe, and Dutch Mennonites opposed violence for any reason. Their members asserted that because Christ forbade war and opposed punishment, they should, too. Members actively sought peaceful solutions to problems. More women than men embraced what was later called pacifism.

The stronger Christianity of any faith became, the more most religious leaders tried to silence women's voices. By the seventeenth century, European governments agreed with the church to suppress women's power, particularly in matters of state. In England and its colonies, married women endured what the law termed civil death. Women had no rights apart from their husbands or fathers.

According to English common law, "Man and wife are one person. . . . To be married, her new self is her superior, her companion, her master."[10] Married women could not sign contracts, keep their earnings, or own property, including possessions that they brought to the marriage. Divorce was granted only in extreme situations, usually to men. Afterwards, children and all belongings went with the father. Women couldn't vote or press charges on their behalf in court.

Only the Society of Friends treated women equally. George and Margaret Fox founded the Society of Friends, or Quakers, in 1652. They had searched for a long time for beliefs that rejected the trappings of traditional religions. The Foxes decided that God lived within the individual, imparting an "inner light." Their followers envisioned a faith that recognized each person's equality before God. All people were created equal, no matter what gender, race, or religion.

Quakers also believed in total nonviolence. They never raised a hand against an enemy in anger, nor did they consider that any reason could justify war. They called themselves Friends because they befriended each other and all humankind. The name Quaker was a disparaging nickname that came either from the Friends' habit of shaking with religious fervor or from a saying of George Fox, "Tremble at the word of the Lord."

Quaker beliefs in equality encouraged women to play an important role in the home and religious community. At religious meetings, women spoke publicly, an unacceptable practice in European society at the time. Women addressed gatherings during services when silent meditation moved them to speak. As Quakerism spread, women took their turn speaking before assemblies of men and serving as ministers and decision makers. The Quaker sense of self-worth and equality produced strong women who later pioneered modern peace movements in Europe and the United States.

Peace groups with revolutionary ideas, such as the Society of Friends, suffered dearly, especially those that granted equal status to women. Men and women experienced mistreatment because of their pacifism. Quakers refused to pay taxes or join armies during wartime. They were branded unpatriotic for their lack of support in battle. Many migrated to the English colonies in North America rather than change their beliefs about equality and peace.

# EARLIEST CALLS FOR PEACE

# 3

*They've taken a notion to speak for themselves,*
*And are wielding the tongue and the pen:*
*They've mounted the rostrum; the (quarrelsome) elves,*
*And—oh Horrid!—are talking to men!*

—Maria Weston Chapman, poet
"The Lords of Creation" (1838)[1]

Seventeenth-century Quaker settlers faced even greater challenges in the American colonies. Problems between Native Americans and colonists frequently turned into warfare. Originally, Native Americans welcomed the Europeans, but they soon discovered that whites held little respect for Indian land and customs. Greedy Europeans broke their word repeatedly, often inciting bloody revenge on both sides. The peace treaties that followed became just another vehicle for whites to make war against Indians by stealing their land.

## COLONIAL DAYS

Several Native American nations listened to the restraining calls for peace from women. Iroquois women preserved a peacekeeping heritage that extended back before settlers arrived. According to tradition, an Iroquois woman was the first person to accept the Great Peace from the prophet Deganawidah.

JIGONSASEE, GREAT PEACE WOMAN, LOOKS OVER THE SHOULDER OF A MODERN IROQUOIS WOMAN IN THIS LINE DRAWING BY TOM HILL.

The woman was known to feed warriors as they passed her wooden longhouse on missions of war. Deganawidah directed the woman to preserve the "Good Tidings of Peace and Power, so that the human race may live in peace in the future."[2] Thereafter, she agreed to stop feeding warriors until the men learned to live in peace. The prophet called this woman Jigonsasee, or New Face, to reflect her

27

new peaceful thinking. He then appointed her the Great Peace Woman, Mother of Nations.

Later generations of Iroquois women followed Great Peace Woman's example. They held the power to choose clan chiefs and decide matters of war and peace. Inheritance passed through the female lines of Iroquois clans. Women planted the fields and controlled the crops. If women withheld food, men didn't go anywhere, including battle. Women assumed a peacekeeping role between warring tribes that wanted to end conflict without losing face.

Colonial peace seekers also encountered the slave trade, which was a booming business. Traders continued to kidnap thousands of Africans for sale at auctions in the colonies, and about one-third of the slaves were women. Once bought, most slaves suffered terrible working and living conditions. Women withstood a double burden: constant work and pregnancies forced on them to produce more slaves. Many women's peace groups would spring from movements opposed to the inhumanity of slavery.

Even more pressing for peace-seeking immigrants was abuse from narrow-minded colonial leaders. Many Puritans, who settled in Massachusetts, had left Europe to follow their own beliefs. Yet Puritans refused to tolerate the views of anyone else. They brought strict views of religion and church authority to the Massachusetts Bay Colony government, including the view that women had no say in church affairs.

In 1634, Anne Hutchinson dared to challenge women's unequal status within the Puritan church. She believed that every person could speak directly with God, thereby bypassing church hierarchy. Hutchinson held weekly discussions with other women to share her beliefs about God and deliver stinging criticism of local ministers. Her meetings became so popular that she reorganized them to include men. By the time authorities heard of Hutchinson, more than 60 men and women attended her talks regularly.

Threatened church leaders brought Hutchinson to

trial. Because church and government were basically the same, she appeared before religious and civil courts. After weeks of questioning and trial, Governor John Winthrop banned Hutchinson from the church and the colony. He charged:

> *Mrs. Hutchinson, you . . . have troubled the peace of the commonwealth and the churches here. You are known to be a woman that hath had a great share in the promoting and divulging of those opinions that are causes of this trouble. . . . It will not well stand with the commonwealth that families should be neglected, for so many neighbors and dames and so much time spent, we see no rule of God for this. . . . We are your judges, and not you ours.*[3]

The only person to speak on Hutchinson's behalf was Mary Dyer, a woman who also paid dearly for her beliefs. Dyer was a Quaker whose peaceful ideas often clashed with colonial views. Quakers in the colonies disapproved of the "Puritan clergy's bloody doctrine of persecution for the cause of conscience."[4] Moreover, Quakers understood that the land belonged to the Indians. Even though this stand was unpopular, Quakers urged colonists to treat Native Americans fairly.

Puritans banned Quakers from Massachusetts Bay Colony between 1654 and 1661 for their "sinful" beliefs. Colonists could be fined 100 pounds for bringing a Quaker into the colony and another 40 shillings for every hour the Quaker stayed. Any Quaker caught in the colony was punished. Quaker women received whippings, jail sentences, ear croppings, and tongue brandings with a hot iron. Repeat offenders faced sale into slavery or the gallows.

Dyer could have lived safely in Rhode Island. Instead, she kept returning to Massachusetts, spreading rebel Quaker teachings about individual self-worth and truth. In 1659, Dyer, 11-year-old Patience Scott, and two men were arrested as they entered Boston. Patience was said to have "an unclean spirit" but was released because of her young age. Dyer was banished "on pain of death" if she returned to Boston.

Seven months later Dyer returned again. This time, Dyer was hanged for the crime of being a Quaker. Years later, the inscription on a statue of her outside the Boston State House read: "A witness for religious freedom: My life not availeth me in comparison to the liberty of the truth."[5]

In 1681, Quaker William Penn founded Pennsylvania as a peaceful colony. The settlement thrived from nonviolent dealings with Native Americans. As the town expanded, many more Quaker women took public stands against colonial violence.

By the early eighteenth century, English tyranny over the colonies overshadowed religious differences. Status for most women remained the same as under English common law. Men still controlled affairs of religion, home, and state. But most colonists, men and women, privately or publicly demanded the right to make judgments about local matters. Many women felt a patriotic duty to rally behind the decision to separate from England.

New England and Mid-Atlantic colonies produced the nation's first nonreligious women's protest groups, in this case against British authority. These women denounced high taxes on British products, such as tea, by refusing to buy them. Many formed anti-tea leagues to promote different ways of brewing tea from raspberry, birch, and sage rather than from British camellia evergreen leaves. They created liberty tea, a popular drink made by boiling the leaves twice and drying them in the oven before brewing.

Some anti-tea leagues united to form the Daughters of Liberty. In 1770, Daughters from 300 Boston families signed a declaration promising not to buy English tea. Other Daughters spun thread and sewed clothes to support boycotts of English cloth products.

By 1775, American colonists declared their independence from Britain, setting off eight years of war. Some pacifist women, such as those who were Mennonites or

Quakers, resisted any action connected with violence. Their families refused to contribute money for supplies to support soldiers, and the men refused to bear arms. Often, these women suffered threats, fines, or beatings for their pacifist views.

Many women, including some in peace churches, chose to support the war in nonviolent ways. Even war was better than British tyranny. During the Battle of Trenton, wives of Quaker soldiers bandaged the wounded on the battlefield. Other women began secret communication networks to transmit war messages or participated in work slowdowns, public protests of British troops, and thefts of British supplies. Mostly, women merely disregarded the British king's orders.

Abigail Adams ran her husband's farm and businesses while he helped plan the new government at the First Continental Congress in Philadelphia. In 1777 she wrote John Adams about a nonviolent women's protest against a storekeeper who hoarded supplies during the war:

> *One eminent, wealthy, stingy merchant (who is a bachelor) had a hogshead of coffee in his store, which he refused to sell the committee under six shillings per pound. A number of females, some say a hundred, some say more, assembled with a cart and trunks, marched down to the warehouse, and demanded the keys . . . then opened the warehouse, hoisted out the coffee themselves, put it into the trunks and drove off. A large concourse of men stood amazed, silent spectators of the whole transaction.*[6]

Lydia Darragh was forced to house British soldiers when they occupied Philadelphia. By chance, she overheard officers plotting a surprise attack against General Washington's camp at White Marsh. Darragh slipped from the city and carried news of the plan to Washington, possibly saving him and the new nation. For her trouble, Darragh's Quaker meeting disowned her and others who placed patriotism over nonviolence. In Philadelphia, several ousted Quakers regrouped into the Free Quakers.

## AFTER THE REVOLUTION

The role women played in the American Revolution served as a model worldwide for individual and mass protests for peace and freedom. Women led bread riots to obtain food before the 1789 French Revolution. They participated in struggles against keeping slaves and serfs in Europe. They challenged colonial rule in Central America, Egypt, and South Africa.

The United States's fight for independence unleashed unprecedented ideas about equality. Americans began to wonder aloud whether a people freed from colonial rule should also free those restricted by its outdated legacy—injustice to women and slaves. Abigail Adams sent special instructions to her husband before he helped draft the Declaration of Independence:

> I long to hear that you have declared an independency. And, by the way, in the new code of laws which I suppose will be necessary for you to make, I desire you would remember the ladies and be more generous and favorable to them than your ancestors. Do not put such unlimited power into the hands of the husbands. Remember, all men would be tyrants if they could. If particular care and attention is not paid to the ladies, we . . . will not hold ourselves bound by any laws in which we have no voice or representation.[7]

Sadly, women received little attention during our nation's founding. Women and their status stayed much the same for decades.

The Revolutionary War thrust the question of slavery into the open for the first time. Slaves had been important to the growth of the colonies, particularly in the South. Slave labor harvested tobacco, produced a profitable south-

ABIGAIL ADAMS WROTE TO HER HUSBAND, JOHN ADAMS, THAT THE DRAFTERS OF THE DECLARATION OF INDEPENDENCE SHOULD "REMEMBER THE LADIES" BY GIVING THEM EQUAL RIGHTS.

ern cotton industry, and expanded the budding nation westward. Slaves toiled on scattered farms and in trade shops in the north, but their numbers and importance to the North's economy were small compared with the South.

During the war, England offered slaves their freedom in exchange for enlisting as British soldiers. Thousands of slaves escaped their owners to fight and later claim their independence. They established communities of free African-Americans throughout the nation. By 1790 almost 60,000 free blacks had built their own schools, churches, and communities to help those still enslaved.

The Revolution sparked hopes among whites and blacks that slavery might be abolished. Over the next 25 years, northern states passed laws and upheld court decisions to free slaves. Despite these calls to end slavery, however, slave labor became more deeply entrenched.

The Constitution had prohibited the slave trade, but not until 1808. Southern plantation owners seized the opportunity to import an additional 40,000 Africans as slaves by the early nineteenth century. Federal law subsequently required the return of any runaway slave over state lines, thereby involving the entire country in slavery. The nation split apart as conflict developed over continuing the horrid system.

One of the first women to protest slavery was a young Quaker named Elizabeth Chandler. At age 18, Chandler wrote poems and articles for the *Genius of Universal Emancipation*, an abolitionist newspaper published by Benjamin Lundy. Chandler's first article urged women to help end the violence of slavery against other women: "Will Christian sisters and wives and mothers stand coldly inert, while those of their own sex are daily exposed, not only to the threats and revilings, but to the very lash of a stern unfeeling taskmaster?"[8]

Chandler died in 1834, but her writings urged women to imagine themselves exposed to the same restraints and violence as slaves. Married women without individual rights began to understand the connection between their lives and those of slave women. Without realizing it, Chandler had laid the groundwork for future women's rights and peace movements.

Scottish-born Frances Wright was another outspoken defender of freedom and equality. At the time, any African blood kept a child from receiving an education. Being female further condemned half the population to lower status. Wright considered the U.S. Constitution a peaceful vehicle for changing these customs. She believed the Constitution guaranteed that nobody would be limited by birth, color, or sex. She argued that free men were themselves lowered when they inflicted lesser status, such as limited rights or education, on others. Wright advocated education for everyone, instead of only wealthy boys. To champion these beliefs, she founded a community called Nashoba in western Tennessee.

More daring than her ideas was Wright's speaking about them in public. Wright was the first woman to speak in public. In 1829, she attracted large audiences of men and women in such major cities as Boston, Baltimore, and St. Louis. Men came to stare and laugh at the oddity of a woman preaching. A few curious women attended Wright's gatherings. Many others agreed with her views but thought attending a pubic display unladylike.

Wright's lectures drew attacks from many fronts—government leaders, churchmen, and the press. One supportive reporter for the *Free Enquirer* wrote, "When Frances Wright explained the nature of knowledge, 'She would repeal the marriage act,' cried the clergy; and when she developed the first principles of moral science, 'She denies the existence of God,' exclaimed the press. . . . Now Frances Wright all this time had said nothing about marriage; never meddled with the Bible, and questioned no man's belief in his God."[9] Extreme ridicule of her programs and public speaking eventually drove Wright from lecture halls.

Similar to Wright, Maria Stewart, an African-American, frequently spoke before Boston audiences. Stewart is considered the first U.S.–born woman to speak before large groups of men and women. Between 1831 and 1833, Stewart gave impassioned pleas to end slavery and educate girls. But like Wright, Stewart's appeals to uplift her people were drowned out by insults hurled against any woman speaking in public.

After two years Stewart stopped the lectures. In her farewell address, she reflected about whether "it is not the color of the skin that makes the man or the woman, but the principle formed in the soul."[10] Even though the women felt defeat, Wright and Stewart broke barriers that gave future peace builders a means of reaching scores of men and women.

# WOMEN AGAINST SLAVERY

# 4

*We Abolition Women are turning the world upside-down.*[1]

—Angelina Grimké

Waves of religious reform swept through early nineteenth-century America, this time involving women. Mothers who could afford the time volunteered for church activities and charity work. With the church's blessing, they formed societies for Bible study and sewing circles. Societies raised money for the poor or for church missionaries, who sought to spread Christianity around the globe.

Meanwhile, local peace groups of mostly men sprang up in response to clashes with England and France. Peace seekers had mistakenly believed that becoming an independent nation, and one separated by oceans from other major powers, would keep war from U.S. shores. Then Great Britain disrupted American shipping, and the resulting War of 1812 shattered the peace seekers' dream.

Peace seekers now actively pressed politicians to resist warfare. Leaders from about 50 local peace groups throughout New England insisted that war was unchristian. In 1828, William Ladd, a Maine farmer and retired sea captain, united several peace organizations into the American

Peace Society. Members agreed that war destroyed people, the economy, and the lives of those who suffered for years to come.

## EARLY WOMEN'S PEACE GROUPS

In a bold move, Ladd encouraged women to join. He emphasized his belief that women were natural peacemakers. Still, Ladd limited women's peacekeeping to traditional arenas of home and church. According to Ladd, women could:

> *pray; educate themselves on peace issues through reading the Bible and peace publications; educate their families by singing peace, not war, songs and reading children stories about peace; refuse to attend military balls; write children's peace literature; join female peace societies and distribute literature; and give their ministers life memberships in peace societies.*[2]

Women's peace groups, such as the Essex County Olive Branch Circle in Massachusetts, emerged as extensions of the men's societies. They centered their activities on charity work and teaching children to seek peace over war. Men in the American Peace Society continued to control decisions related to national and international affairs. Yet a growing number of women, such as Elizabeth Chandler, reached audiences of men and women with writings about various peace issues.

A fiery pacifist and printer named William Lloyd Garrison joined the American Peace Society. But Garrison soon found the group moved too slowly toward change for his taste. In sharp contrast to Ladd's goal of gradually ending slavery, Garrison believed in immediate justice, and his demand for equal status for women and slaves clashed with Ladd's view of limited participation by women.

Those who agreed with Garrison to resist any form of violence formed the New England Non-Resistance Society.

This became the most outspoken peace group before the Civil War. The society gained attention for its large number of female members. Women were also officers, a first among coed organizations.

## ANTISLAVERY WOMEN

In 1831, Garrison founded the New England Anti-Slavery Society to focus on ending slavery. He published the *Liberator* as the group's weekly voice of peace and equality. A special column, the "Ladies Department," guaranteed expression of women's opinions. Garrison marked the column with a sketch of a slave woman on her knees in chains. A heading above the picture asked, "Am I Not a Woman and a Sister?"[3]

Despite Garrison's pleas, the New England Anti-Slavery Society remained a male-run organization. Women attended the first meeting by invitation, and Quaker abolitionist Lucretia Mott addressed the group. But most members claimed women were unsuited to join or sign the "Declaration of Sentiments and Purposes." After the meeting, 20 women banded together to establish the Philadelphia Female Anti-Slavery Society, with Mott as president.

Forty-year-old Mott seemed unruffled in her role as a leader of a revolutionary woman's group. As a Quaker, she was already an experienced leader. Her calm speeches and profound faith in Quaker peaceful teachings earned her respect from the angriest audiences. Mott believed her job was to foster peace and nonresistance, at all costs.

Privately, Mott never bought products made by slaves. Her husband James, a successful merchant, refused to sell cotton because it came from slave labor. The Mott home was a safe hideaway for runaway slaves traveling the Underground Railroad, a secret network along the route to freedom in Canada. Individuals who dared take a stand against slavery faced great opposition. Mott's friends snubbed her, while strangers shouted insults. Even caring Quakers scolded her for constantly bringing up slavery at their meet-

Lucretia Mott, a Quaker leader, lectured widely against slavery and for women's rights.

ings and wished she would resign her post. Yet Mott remained fearless.

At one antislavery meeting, hostile mobs surrounded Pennsylvania Hall as Mott addressed a gathering of women. Men hurled bricks and stones through the window. Their shouts drowned out her words. Mott calmly led a chain of women holding hands to safety. But the mob set the empty hall aflame and headed toward the Mott house. Luckily, a family friend steered the angry crowd in the wrong direction.

Even with constant threats, Mott stood firm in her belief in nonviolence. She declared:

> *Misrepresentation and ridicule and abuse heaped on these reforms do not in the least deter me from my duty. . . . I have no idea, because I am a Non-Resistant [someone who refuses to fight under any conditions, even when attacked], of submitting tamely to injustice inflicted either on me or the slave. I will oppose it with all the moral powers with which I am endowed.[4]*

Women throughout New England organized their own antislavery societies. Maria Weston Chapman, a Garrison abolitionist, helped establish the Boston Female Anti-Slavery Society. Freed African-American women organized the First Female Anti-Slavery Society in Salem, Massachusetts. Similar societies formed in most major cities in the North and West.

New antislavery groups gave women a reason to move beyond the home in larger numbers. Proper abolitionist ladies raised money by holding "antislavery fairs," where they sold handmade goods. Decorative needlework made into bags, books, pincushions, and banners was inscribed with messages against slavery. "May the points of our needles prick the slaveholders conscience," read the handiwork of Northern children.[5]

Bolder women, black and white, opened their homes as Underground Railroad stations. Of these "conductors," Harriet Tubman became the most renowned. As a slave who escaped north to freedom, Tubman was troubled about the friends and relatives she left behind in Maryland. Tubman returned south to lead runaway slaves along the dangerous Underground Railroad. She risked her life to save more than 300 people, which earned her the nickname Moses, the name of the Jewish prophet who led his people from slavery in Egypt.

The abolition movement encouraged women to become activists. They held public meetings for the first time and wrote and sold antislavery pamphlets. Societies gathered hundreds of names during door-to-door petition drives. Petitions called for new states to be free from slavery and protested the sale of slaves across state lines. By 1834, petition drives proved so successful that threatened Southern congressmen, who defended slavery, introduced a bill to the U.S. House of Representatives that outlawed petitions.

Speaking against slavery grew more dangerous, especially for women. Few females other than Quakers and Maria Stewart had spoken in public since Ann Hutchinson's failed attempt 200 years earlier. Women offended listeners with their nonviolent ideas and with their "unwomanly" public lectures. Antislavery women dared to address mixed audiences of men and women, blacks and whites.

Angelina and Sarah Grimké refused to keep silent while other women feared for their lives under slavery. The Grimkés, daughters of South Carolina slaveholders, despised slavery. Sarah accompanied her sick father to Philadelphia for medical care. After he died, she was attracted to Quaker ideals of human rights. Sarah attended the lectures of Lucretia Mott and others, and she decided to stay in Philadelphia. Within a few years, Sarah's younger sister Angelina joined her and the Quakers.

The sisters agreed to tell others about the shameful conditions that they had witnessed in the South. In 1836 the Grimkés published a series of heartrending pamphlets. Angelina wrote "An Appeal to the Christian Women of the South," which questioned how slave-owning women could tolerate other women being chained and beaten. Angelina urged Southern wives to persuade their husbands that slavery was horrible. Further, she encouraged readers to free slaves they owned, educate them, and see them safely out of the slave states—even if these actions were unlawful. "Wicked laws ought to be no barrier," was her call to nonviolent action.[6]

Rather than spread the word in the Grimkés' home state of South Carolina, postmasters burned the writings. The Charleston mayor threatened to jail or mob the women if they returned home. But Garrison gladly printed Angelina's writings for the *Liberator*'s 1,000 subscribers to read.

The next year the Grimkés and other antislavery women spoke before the first national convention of U.S. women abolitionists in New York City. More than 200 women from 10 states listened to speeches demanding race and gender justice. The speakers based their arguments on the popular notion that women are peaceful, nonviolent guardians of society, while men are frequently the reverse.

Northern antislavery societies heard of the sisters and invited them to address their members. The Grimkés launched a tour of the Northeast to tell gatherings of women about the shameful lives slaves were forced to lead. Curious audiences expanded into the hundreds, with men joining the women. In 1838 the Grimké sisters told five hundred people in the Boston State House about the evils of slavery. They became the first women to address the Massachusetts House of Representatives—or any state legislature.

Interest in the Grimkés brought widespread attacks from Southerners and Northern textile industrialists who owned slaves. The worst charges came from churches. Massachusetts clergy issued a letter attacking their opinions as unladylike and unchristian. They claimed that "when a woman assumes the place and tone of man as public reformer . . . her character becomes unnatural."[7]

Sarah Grimké was outraged at the charges. She argued that clergy distorted the Bible to keep women in their place. She accused all men of trying to "crush the immortal mind of woman." Sarah further linked the position of women to that of slaves: "All I ask of our brethren is that they will take their feet off our necks and permit us to stand upright on that ground which God designed us to occupy."[8]

Never before had women questioned their lack of rights in public. Now women understood that in order to help free slaves they must be free also. Early antislavery women laid the foundation for a flood of women working together for equal rights and freedom.

Some joined female moral reform societies to publicly expose men's injustice toward women. Reform society women spied on brothels, keeping track of men who visited the women inside. Then they published names of men who entered to embarrass them. These were some of the earliest organized demonstrations by women and for women in the United States.

Seeds of the first major women's rights movement were planted at the 1840 World Anti-Slavery Convention in England. Lucretia Mott attended the conference as part of the U.S. delegation. In London, Mott met American Elizabeth Cady Stanton, a thoughtful, strong-willed younger woman, who was on a honeymoon with her abolitionist husband, Henry Stanton. When Mott, Stanton, and two other female delegates arrived at the convention, they discovered that only men were allowed a seat and full participation. The women protested, and a vote was taken. But old ideas that women belonged at home and not in public affairs persisted. Male delegates informed the women they could sit in the gallery or leave.

Garrison appeared a few days later to find the women seated in the gallery. He was so outraged he joined the women upstairs. Over much objection, Mott finally received permission to speak at a tea for 400 delegates. Her stirring words aroused applause from the same admirers who continued to exclude her from the convention.

During the convention Mott and Stanton formed a close bond. They discussed the meetings and how women

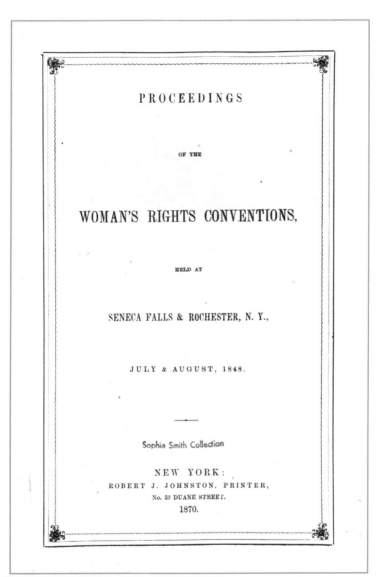

PROCEEDINGS

OF THE

WOMAN'S RIGHTS CONVENTIONS,

HELD AT

SENECA FALLS & ROCHESTER, N. Y.,

JULY & AUGUST, 1848.

Sophia Smith Collection

NEW YORK:
ROBERT J. JOHNSTON, PRINTER,
No. 59 DUANE STREET.
1870.

THE TITLE PAGE OF THE PROCEEDINGS OF THE 1848
SENECA FALLS RIGHTS CONVENTION. AT THE
CONVENTION, 68 WOMEN AND 32 MEN SIGNED A
DECLARATION DETAILING THE INJUSTICES AGAINST WOMEN
AND METHODS TO REMEDY THEM.

could organize to prevent their rights being taken away again. Eight years later, their vision of a women's gathering developed into the groundbreaking Seneca Falls Women's Rights Convention.

On July 19, 1848, more than 300 people attended the meeting at a chapel in Seneca Falls, New York. Of these, 68 women and 32 men signed the Declaration of Sentiments, a list of injustices against women and ways to remedy them. The women modeled the document after the Declaration of Independence and the New England Non-Resistance Society's Sentiments, which rejected any government that tolerates war. The Declaration of Sentiments began:

> *When in the course of human events, it becomes necessary for one portion of the family of man to assume among the people of the earth a position different from that which they have hitherto occupied . . . But when a long train of abuses . . . . to reduce [women] under absolute despotism, it is their duty to throw off such government, and to provide new guards for their future security.*[9]

Abolitionist women successfully connected the need for peace with demands for women's political rights as citizens. Without equal rights, women had little power to influence greater issues of slavery, war, and peace. The Seneca Falls convention launched a rush of meetings and speaking tours to gain property rights, child custody, divorce, education, and more important, the right to vote.

Women's rights took a back seat when the Civil War erupted in 1861. Many women put aside their demands for equal rights and shouldered jobs, replacing men who joined the army. Some women dressed as soldiers and went into battle; others provided relief by cooking and sewing for the army or bandaging the injured.

With this war, however, women assumed more risks and entered occupations previously closed to them. Greater numbers of women became teachers, nurses, and industrial and government workers. Even those opposed to war appreciated the value of the opportunities given women to control money and think about politics.

Garrison and the American Peace Society declared that President Lincoln was right to defend the U.S. government. Although they hated violence, women and men who shared Garrison's views hoped war would finally free the slaves.

Lucretia Mott and other strict pacifists took a principled stand against any violence. Mott helped organize the Woman's Association for the Aid of Freedmen in Philadelphia. Her support went to freed slaves and conscientious objectors, men who refused to fight on moral grounds. Mott believed, "Women as well as men are interested in these works of justice and mercy. . . . The blessing to the merciful, to the peacemaker is equal to man and to woman."[10]

Elizabeth Cady Stanton and Susan B. Anthony formed the Woman's National Loyal League in 1863. Anthony was a Quaker who devoted her life to humane causes. She had lectured against slavery and later worked to end the flow of alcohol, which sometimes triggered violence at home.

Anthony first met Stanton in 1850. Their association led to the fight for suffrage, the right to vote. Now Anthony and Stanton organized volunteers into the Loyal League for an antislavery petition drive. The league sought three million signatures for a constitutional amendment to abolish slavery forever. They further hoped Congress would approve a similar amendment to give women the vote.

Within a year, Loyal League members collected nearly 400,000 signatures. Two freed slaves presented large bundles of petition rolls to Massachusetts senator Charles Sumner, who lugged a sampling to President Lincoln. The petition fell short of the original goal, yet the huge number of signatures demonstrated the power of women working together for change.

By the close of the war, women peace seekers deepened their conviction that lasting peace depended upon their

47

SUSAN B. ANTHONY (STANDING) AND ELIZABETH CADY STANTON WORKED TOGETHER IN THE WOMEN'S MOVEMENT FOR MANY YEARS. DURING THE CIVIL WAR, THEY FOUNDED THE WOMAN'S LOYAL LEAGUE, WHICH ORGANIZED A COLOSSAL ANTISLAVERY PETITION DRIVE.

achieving equal rights. Mott, Stanton, and their co-workers officially claimed peace as a women's issue. Lucretia Mott worked through the Universal Peace Union that she and other women helped found in 1866, as well as the local Pennsylvania Peace Society. The Universal Peace Union showed concern for issues beyond warring nations. Members linked war with racial and economic injustice. They rallied on behalf of any group that was treated unfairly— African-Americans, Native Americans, recent European and Asian immigrants, and women.

Mott and other Universal Peace Union representatives introduced several positions still held today. They spoke against war toys for children and school textbooks that glorified war. They opposed the death penalty for criminals. The union also urged an end to military training in schools, a program that survived in high schools until the 1960s.

Although Mott devoted most of her 85 years to peace groups, she continued to support the women's vote as a means to ensure peace. "Place woman in equal power, and you will find her capable of not abusing it. . . . Give her the privilege to cooperate in making the laws she submits to, and there will be harmony without severity and justice without oppression."[11]

Stanton took a stronger position against men's ability to keep peace. She saw men as greedy, violent creatures who loved power, conquest, and the glory of battle. For her, women brought "purity, virtue, morality, true religion, to lift man up into higher realms of thought and action."[12] Moreover, Stanton envisioned a broader peacekeeping mission for women, one that accepted the bond among all peoples. With this vision came the hope for a new era of international peace.

# WORLDWIDE CAMPAIGN 5

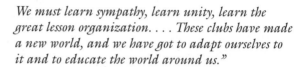

*We must learn sympathy, learn unity, learn the great lesson organization. . . . These clubs have made a new world, and we have got to adapt ourselves to it and to educate the world around us."*

—Mary Eastman,
New England Women's Club[1]

Julia Ward Howe, writer and suffragist, shared Elizabeth Cady Stanton's desire for a global women's peace movement. For years, Howe lived an isolated life in a stifling marriage. Occasionally she occupied herself by writing poems or plays. Her poem "Battle Hymn of the Republic" was published in the February 1862 *Atlantic Monthly* and later set to the tune "John Brown's Body." The moving song inspired the war-weary North, making Howe a celebrity. Howe used this newfound fame to focus attention on her true concerns: women's rights and peace.

When France and Germany clashed in 1870, Howe was horrified at yet another war. She quickly wrote "Appeal to Womanhood throughout the World," an antiwar article that called on women everywhere "to unite across national borders to prevent the waste of human life which they alone bear and know the cost."[2] Two years later, Howe sailed for London. Her dream was to build a Woman's Peace Congress that would cooperate with a meeting of world leaders. But British peace officials refused to deal with a woman, and few females had the finances and time to join the congress.

Howe returned home still determined to organize women for peace on a grand scale. Her next plan was to hold a national peace day honoring mothers, people who understood the suffering caused by war. Through letters, petitions, and meetings, Howe recruited women for spring Women's Peace Festivals. She held the festivals at varied locations for women unable to travel. Written notices went to clergy, teachers, and newspapers about programs occurring in churches, synagogues, schools, and universities. In each, Howe stressed the importance of honoring peacemakers rather than military heroes.

In June 1873, Mothers' Peace Day celebrations occurred in several U.S. cities and overseas in Manchester, London, Geneva, Rome, and Constantinople. Hundreds of women gathered to express their hatred of war and military training for boys. Participants used the occasion to press for the right of women to vote to keep peace. Women's groups celebrated similar Peace Day festivals each June 2 for the next 36 years.

## A SMALL VOICE IS HEARD

Conditions during the late nineteenth century freed many more women for peace work. Inventions of gas lights, ice production, indoor plumbing, improved sewing machines, and food canning devices lessened the time women spent with household chores. A wave of unskilled immigrant women accepted low-paying jobs as nursemaids and cooks, permitting women who could afford help a chance to escape the grind of housework.

Scattered breakthroughs gave women broader leadership skills for peace activities by the early twentieth century. Women gained complete voting rights in Wyoming (1870) and Utah (1896) and the power to select candidates for specific local offices in several other states. Gradually, individual states passed laws recognizing a woman's rights to own property, keep her wages, make a will, and gain custody of children and inheritance.

Coed colleges, such as Oberlin, and new women's universities—such as Vassar, Bryn Mawr, and Wellesley in the East and Jacksonville in Illinois—paved the way for higher learning. Even though female workers remained undervalued for the next century, more women entered professions as doctors, journalists, lawyers, business owners, and teachers. Between 1870 and 1890, the number of women physicians rose from 544 to 4,500, and the number of teachers increased from 90,000 to 250,000.[3]

Similarly, women from poorer families found acceptance earning wages outside the home. In 1850, 50 percent of the one million factory workers were women, which was 10 percent of the total wage earners. Thereafter, many women moved from farms to factory towns looking for work and migrated westward to settle homesteads and mining towns. By 1900, women outnumbered men in some industries, particularly clothes manufacturing. Twenty percent of the nation's workforce involved women who ran boardinghouses or who were servants, factory and mill workers, professionals, laundresses, seamstresses, and salesclerks.

Women's emerging community involvement opened opportunities in peace groups. The American Peace Society voted to allow women officers in 1871. By the 1890s, 50 percent of Universal Peace Union (UPU) members, as well as one-third of its leaders, were women.

Belva Lockwood was one of the most outspoken UPU officers. Lockwood was the first woman lawyer allowed to practice before the United States Supreme Court, in 1879. She used this privilege in 1906 to represent the Eastern Cherokee Nation in several court battles, gaining them money for past injustices. Her greatest fame, however, came when she ran twice for the presidency as the candidate for the National Equal Rights Party. In 1884, Lockwood received only about four thousand votes from six states,

In 1884, a group of Rahway, New Jersey, men attempt to ridicule Belva Ann Lockwood, presidential candidate of the National Equal Rights Party, by parading in Mother Hubbard outfits. The crowd laughed at the men instead of Lockwood.

and she tallied even fewer votes in 1888. Still, many women applauded her courage.

Several women-only societies, clubs, and suffrage organizations brought networks of people together to make peace an important issue. Women's club programs in large cities worked for better child care, health care, and factory conditions and for social reform to establish more peaceful communities. The Grange, or Patrons of Husbandry, brought organized farm women together to seek equal status. Upper-class Southern women, who had their sheltered plantation world shattered by the Civil War, found women's clubs safe vehicles for exploring broader programs.

One of the largest networks of women's clubs was the National Association of Colored Women (NACW). Although most white women's societies began as religious, sewing, or book clubs, black women organized around causes to free and better their people. The Civil War hardly improved the imbalance of rights accorded blacks and whites.

Former slave Sojourner Truth risked her life time and again to gain equal status with whites. She boarded segregated railroad trolleys and fearlessly confronted angry conductors, who forced her out of seats reserved for whites only. After several incidents, Truth brought a successful lawsuit against the city of Washington, D.C., to end segregated trolleys. Truth remembered: "before the trial was ended, the inside of cars looked like salt and I felt like Poll Parrot, [saying] 'Jack, I am riding.' "[4]

## LOUDER CALLS AGAINST VIOLENCE

After the Civil War many southern whites resisted blacks' gaining power. Violence and threats of lynching increased. For postwar African-Americans, peace meant survival and freedom from Ku Klux Klan terror. The threat of this violent hate group reached into northern states as well.

In some northern areas, even successful African-Americans were considered second-class citizens. As one club member observed, black women's groups represented "the organized anxiety of women who have become intelligent enough to realize their own low condition, and strong enough to initiate the forces of reform.[5]

Ida B. Wells, an African-American teacher, organizer, and writer, used her pen to promote justice and nonviolence. In 1889, Wells became part-owner and editor of the Memphis *Free Speech*. Her first articles criticized substandard Memphis schools for African-American children. Publication of these articles abruptly ended her teaching career.

Wells next tackled white lynch mobs that targeted blacks. She studied records of 726 lynchings of black men and women over 10 years. Many of the incidents involved fake claims of white women being raped by black men. The inquiry confirmed her belief that the murders were just another means of restoring white power in the South. Equally alarming was the amount of sexual violence by white men against black women that went unchallenged. Because whites controlled the police and government, blacks had no recourse under law.[6]

In 1892 alone, the number of reported lynchings soared to 241. The same year, lynchers used rape charges to mask the real reason that they hung three of Wells's friends: their thriving black-owned People's Grocery Company threatened white shopkeepers. Wells blasted the mob in a *Free Speech* editorial, charging rape was used as an excuse for violence. White citizens responded by destroying Wells's office while she was in New York. Afterward, a Memphis newspaper printed a front-page story demanding that "the black wretch who had written that foul lie be tied to a stake . . . and publicly burned."[7]

While exiled from Memphis, Wells launched a series of antilynching articles and lectures. Her crusade led to the founding of black women's clubs in Boston and New York, and throughout the Midwest. Most allied with the National Association of Colored Women. Wells later championed a black boycott of Atlanta street cars. Her reactions against hate crimes and sexual assaults provided the basis for future civil rights activities against violence.

Native American women suffered similar violence because of their race and gender. Settlers pushed west, building towns, laying train tracks, and stringing telegraph wires. Few cared that Native Americans had lived on the same land for centuries before Europeans arrived. Indian nations lost their homeland, population, and way of life, only to be forced onto barren reservation land. Tribes that fought removal had little chance of winning, let alone surviving.

According to the Dakota, one woman brought peace

during the late nineteenth century, at least among Native American nations. Tailfeather Woman gave her people the sacred Drum Dance. As U.S. soldiers attacked her people, Tailfeather Woman fled into a lake and hid under a lily pad. While in hiding, Tailfeather Woman received the sacred teachings from the Great Spirit.

These teachings sought to establish peace and end bloodshed. Tailfeather Woman shared them with other Native American communities in the form of songs, rituals, and ceremonies. Each honored the Drum Dance and the Great Spirit. Even though wars with soldiers continued, the Drum Dance promoted brotherhood and peace among tribes throughout the Great Plains.

The United States's desire for new territory led to many disputes beyond its borders. During the last half of the nineteenth century, U.S. soldiers invaded Latin America more than 20 times. In 1893, U.S. marines overthrew the Hawaiian government of Queen Liliuokalani. After each invasion, U.S. leaders claimed the attacks were necessary to guard the country's business interests and support friendly governments.

Suffragist Lillie Devereux Blake addressed 1,000 members of the National American Woman Suffrage Association, the leading women's group dedicated to securing the woman's vote. Her 1896 speech about the status of peace attacked men for their "inability to settle conflict without violence and their willingness to deluge the world in blood for a strip of land in Venezuela or a gold mine in South Africa."[8]

## THE TEMPERANCE MOVEMENT AND PEACE

One of the most active groups to call for peace was the Woman's Christian Temperance Union (WCTU). The WCTU had been founded in 1874 to protest increased alcohol production after the Civil War. Temperance workers argued that the government, which received money from alcohol taxes, overlooked problems the sinful drink caused for families.

MEMBERS OF THE WOMEN'S CHRISTIAN TEMPERANCE UNION (WCTU) IN MORO, OREGON, POSED FOR THIS 1890 GROUP PHOTO. ALTHOUGH THE WCTU WAS FOUNDED TO COMBAT THE EVILS OF ALCOHOL, THE ORGANIZATION ALSO CONFRONTED THE ISSUES OF WAR AND VIOLENCE

Frances Willard, WCTU's forceful president, believed that alcohol and militarism were naturally linked. Both caused violence, and both affected mostly men. Willard introduced programs that combined ending the sale of alcohol with issues of war and violence.

Under Willard's direction, Hannah Bailey, a Maine

Quaker minister and active peace worker, created the WCTU's Department of Peace and Arbitration in 1887. For the next six years, WCTU members prepared lectures and booklets condemning war toys, high school military drills, draft for soldiers, lynchings, and boxing matches. Bailey directed publication of two monthly peace journals: *Acorn* focused on children, and *Pacific Banner* was for adults. The WCTU held children's programs on Peace Sundays that included youth peace bands and clubs.

Anything that purged the world of evil and fostered Christian goodness and home life became part of WCTU programs. WCTU women glorified motherhood and the "ideal of mother love." One WCTU brochure read: "It is the duty of the mother to prevent quarrels, likewise to make peace where contentions exist."[9]

By 1889, Bailey extended her department throughout the WCTU international organization. Peace, suffrage, nonviolence, and religion were spread worldwide by female temperance workers. Sometimes WCTU representatives joined with other local and national women's groups. The WCTU allowed women to become involved in foreign policy on a grand scale for the first time. Women's voices denounced the U.S. war against Chile in 1891. They protested England's dispute with Venezuela four years later.

## THE SPANISH-AMERICAN WAR

The 1898 Spanish-American War was a major blow to peace seekers. The United States supported Cuba's independence from Spain because it opened opportunities for trade and influence in Latin America. President William McKinley assumed he could intervene between Spain and Cuba and prevent a crisis. After Spain turned down his attempts, McKinley ordered the battleship *Maine* to Havana. He claimed that he merely wanted to protect U.S. lives and property. Seven days later the ship exploded, killing 260 people.

McKinley suspected the blast was Spain's doing. After

another attempt to negotiate with Spain failed, he declared war. In the end, the United States triumphed. Cuba was free, and the United States gained colonies in Guam, Puerto Rico, and the Philippine Islands. The victory also proved that the United States was now an international military power.

The war shocked large numbers of pacifists into action. Many more women joined ongoing social reform groups or organized new peace groups. A network of peace organizations formed on college campuses. The old American Peace Society sprang back to life. In 1908, Fanny Fern Andrews created the American School Peace League in Boston. Her group was dedicated to teaching children about worldwide harmony.

Leading women suffragists used their networks to promote world peace. Peace organizations comprised mostly white, middle-class, and Christian women; however, strong support came from the National Council of Negro Women and the National Council of Jewish Women. Much like Elizabeth Cady Stanton before them, women in these groups held a common belief that men caused war because they were innately violent, competitive, and money-hungry.

Among women's groups, opinions varied about whether to aid Cuba. Nonetheless, the fighting continued for more than a year. In the end, America lost 5,462 lives, and the war cost $283.2 million.

Then U.S. troops brutally crushed a Philippine movement for independence. Angry pacifists opposed the idea of any nation forcing itself on another. The Colorado WCTU circulated petitions against killing Filipinos because they wanted their freedom.

Peace workers agreed that winning the Spanish-American War had strengthened male greed for new possessions. Yet the WCTU and other groups offered a model for a women's international peace organization.

# BIRTH OF THE WOMEN'S PEACE MOVEMENT

6

*For the Safety of the Nation*
*To the Women Give the Vote.*
*For the Hand that Rocks the Cradle*
*Will Never Rock the Boat.*

—Republican National Convention
suffrage banner[1]

G rowing interest in a women's organization for world peace led to the 1899 Hague Conference. The meeting developed from efforts of the International Congress of Women, a global suffrage group. Julia Ward Howe had addressed the congress's first meeting in 1888, hoping members would adopt a peace platform. Those who attended in 1888 preferred to stress a woman's right to vote, but they agreed to link voting to a program for women's political equality and more humane government. Following this plan, the Washington branch adopted the familiar Golden Rule: "Do onto others as they would do unto you."

Womens' groups throughout the United States supported the 1899 international peace conference. Suffragists in the National American Woman Suffrage Association and National Council of Women held educational meetings about the conference for their members. Meanwhile, social reform groups, such as the General Federation of Women's Clubs and the National Council of Jewish Women, informed the general public. The response was heartening. The *Woman's Tribune,* published by the Nebraska Woman's Suffrage Association, reported that more than 90 towns in Utah alone held meetings to promote the Hague Conference.[2]

The actual conference proved a strong first step toward an international voice for women's issues. Participants came from Great Britain, Ireland, Wales, the United States, Germany, Sweden, Canada, Tasmania, New Zealand, Holland, and Denmark. They represented groups totaling more than six million women. Julia Howe, then 80 years old and too frail to attend, was proud to learn that the gathering included so many women who were "all aware of the issues of war, peace, woman suffrage, and violence against women."[3]

## THE ECONOMY AS A PEACE ISSUE

During the early twentieth century, peace work took its place alongside many social reforms of the day. Jane Addams founded Chicago's Hull House and Lillian Wald opened New York's Henry House, two of the first settlement houses in the nation. These women created safe havens for the poor while fighting battles on their behalf with city governments and industrial giants. Through their work among the poor, they and other reformers sounded the earliest alarms about widespread problems of child labor, horrible factory conditions, unsanitary housing, and mistreatment of immigrant workers.

Social reformers noted that the Industrial Revolution had generated great wealth for only a few men and their families. At the same time, industry profits came at the expense of workers who were often abused. Addams concluded that "there could be no peace without social and economic justice."[4] The social reform movement that followed raised nonviolent peace activities, once the crusade of traditional peace churches, to public concerns.

Suffrage groups continued to press for the vote as a way to end violence. But life seemed to leave the suffrage movement after many of its colorful leaders—Elizabeth Stanton, Lucretia Mott, and Susan B. Anthony—died. Carrie Chapman Catt had led the National American Woman Suffrage Association through early victories, but she left the organization to tend her sick husband and to organize an international suffrage group.

Factory workers took the lead in calling for better conditions for women. Through their "unladylike" public actions, factory workers changed the way women battled unfair treatment. In 1909 and 1910, women workers organized major strikes against manufacturers in Philadelphia, Chicago, and New York. Women dared to walk out on bosses and form picket lines until their demands were met. Striking marchers carried banners that told onlookers, "We Strike for Justice."

Reports of the strikes, and the terrible working conditions that prompted them, drew considerable female support. New unions formed, and existing ones, such as the New York Women's Trade Union League and the International Ladies Garment Workers Union, swelled with added members. Wealthy women donated money for bail and aid to striking families. Many women suffragists and peace workers joined picket lines to replace arrested strikers who sought better working conditions.

In 1910 female factory workers and suffragists united to plan the first suffrage parade in New York City. Rows of suffragists wearing yellow "Votes for Women" sashes marched up Fifth Avenue beside their working sisters. Colorful banners and flags attracted crowds of busy shoppers. The parade proved so successful that it became an annual event. After the third parade, the *New York Times* reported "20,000 marchers and 500,000 onlookers."[5] With these bold actions, women peace seekers learned how to demand attention for their cause.

## THE NOBEL PEACE PRIZE

At the same time, some wealthy businessmen contributed to peace movements. Sweden's Alfred Nobel, who had

IN 1905, BERTHA VON SUTTNER WON THE FIRST NOBEL
PEACE PRIZE EVER AWARDED TO A WOMAN.

earned his fortune from manufacturing dynamite and died
in 1896, established the Nobel Peace Prize in his will. The
prize, first awarded in 1901, honored individuals whose
major achievements advanced peace. A committee, which
sometimes included women, selected winners from among

those nominated by individuals or groups worldwide. Initial prizes went to trailblazers of organized peace groups.

The first woman to receive the Nobel Peace Prize was German journalist Bertha von Suttner in 1905. Baroness von Suttner had inspired her friend Nobel to include a peace prize in his will. But she earned the prize in her own right as a dynamic writer and lecturer who championed negotiation and total disarmament.

Von Suttner wrote the popular antiwar novel *Lay Down Your Arms*. The book was compared to Harriet Beecher Stowe's *Uncle Tom's Cabin*, about the evils of slavery. Both novels increased popular support for important peace issues. Von Suttner founded the German Peace Society to back her peace campaigns.

## WORLD WAR I

American women's clubs retained their importance in organizing women. By 1914, the General Federation of Women's Clubs claimed 800,000 members. Large memberships remained in the Council of Mothers (100,000), Women's Relief Corps (161,000), WCTU (325,000), and the 15 clubs within the National Council of Women. Each declared that their members supported peace. Yet there was still no single women's peace association.[6]

On August 4, 1914, war erupted in Europe. At first, most Americans opposed U.S. involvement. President Woodrow Wilson declared the United States neutral, assuring the country and foreign leaders that he wanted to help restore peace. By 1915, stories of brutal German invasions of Belgium began to sway public opinion toward the Allies—France, England, and Russia—and against the Central Powers of Germany, Austria-Hungary, Bulgaria, and Turkey.

Women peace seekers expected strong stands from long-running male-led peace groups. But male pacifist leaders seemed reluctant to suggest that the United States should stay out of the war. Concerned women formed a

Peace Parade Committee. They wanted to hold a rally that would reflect their anger yet show support for American neutrality.

Prominent women's rights leaders, social reformers, and pacifists arranged a massive demonstration in New York City. The committee's leader was Fanny Garrison Villard, the 70-year-old daughter of outspoken pacifist William Lloyd Garrison. Villard hoped the Peace Parade Committee would evolve into an all-women peace organization separate from traditional suffrage activities.

On August 29, 1914, more than 1,500 women marched down Fifth Avenue, much like their suffrage and factory-worker sisters before them. Only these women paraded silently in mourning clothes to the steady pounding of drums. Their banners displayed doves holding an olive branch as a sign of peace. Although the parade drew attention to the possibility of war, no new women's peace group emerged. Still, the *New York Times* recognized the women as an outspoken voice in matters of war.

Within a few months, English peace advocate Emmeline Pethick-Lawrence and Rosika Schwimmer, a Hungarian suffragist and journalist, joined forces for a U.S. speaking tour. These women from opposing countries wanted U.S. suffragists to urge their neutral government to mediate a peace settlement. Pethick-Lawrence and Schwimmer persuaded a group of well-known reformers that it was their job as women to reestablish peace.

Jane Addams, Lillian Wald, labor defender Crystal Eastman, and Carrie Chapman Catt called a meeting of 26 women's-group representatives for January 10, 1915. Catt later remembered: "When the great war came, and the women waited for the pacifists to move, and they heard nothing from them, they decided all too late to get together themselves and try to do something at this eleventh hour."[7] From this meeting came the Woman's Peace Party (WPP), the first major independent women's peace group.

The Woman's Peace Party prepared the most extreme platform of any peace group to date. The women called for

A CROWD OF WOMEN LISTEN TO A PANEL DISCUSSION AT
THE 1915 WOMEN'S PEACE CONGRESS.

a voice in foreign policy and measures to control arms and their manufacture. Peace Party women pledged to educate children for peace and eliminate economic causes of war. Once again, women linked the causes of peace and suffrage. Peace seekers insisted that "women must be given a share in deciding between war and peace in all courts of high debate—within the home, the school, the church, the industrial order, and the state."[8]

Immediately, Schwimmer presented President Wilson with a petition that recommended he arrange a meeting of neutral nations. University of Wisconsin instructor Julia Wales drafted a list of peace terms. On an international level, 47 Woman's Peace Party members traveled to the Hague in April 1915. They met with more than 1,500 representatives from 12 neutral and warring countries at another International Congress of Women. Jane Addams, the impartial Woman's Peace Party chairwoman, was asked to preside over the four-day congress.

The 1915 Hague conference resulted in a strong desire to continue a global exchange through the Women's International Committee for Permanent Peace, with headquarters in Amsterdam. The Woman's Peace Party formed the United States division. Jane Addams led delegates to meet with heads of eight warring European countries and President Wilson.

According to Addams in *Women at the Hague*, the women offered a peace plan that pressed leaders for "negotiations which must in the end take place unless the war shall continue year after year and at last be terminated through sheer exhaustion."[9] Although several officials agreed with the women, none would commit to beginning the peace process.

At home, Wilson remained unresponsive. Schwimmer convinced car tycoon Henry Ford to charter the cruise ship *Oscar II* for a U.S. peace delegation abroad. Ford dubbed the project, "get the boys out of the trenches by Christmas." Still, the president refused to support Ford's project or U.S. intervention. The press ridiculed women and men who planned to sail, and they and Ford were eventually forced to abandon the trip.[10]

Government agents harassed Woman's Peace Party members regularly. Nasty press coverage dogged party women, especially Jane Addams. They were attacked as meddling in affairs that didn't concern women and branded as unpatriotic.

On May 7, 1915, German submarines sank the British ocean liner *Lusitania*, killing 128 U.S. citizens. The mood in Washington and the nation shifted toward readiness for war. Still, the women persisted in attacking war as wasting money that could be better spent for social reform. The determined Addams met with President Wilson six times between July and December to insist that he seek negotiation. By 1916, Woman's Peace Party membership climbed to a high of 40,000, with 165 separate groups nationwide.

The women devised new plans to oppose arming U.S. soldiers. The Peace Party distributed pamphlets challenging arms buildup and military training in school. Frances Witherspoon helped organize the New York Bureau of Legal Advice for men who wanted to refuse military service. Addams testified against increased military spending before a congressional committee.

The New York City branch, the most active in the Woman's Peace Party, took the fight to the streets. In early 1916, members held mass meetings at Cooper Union to protest promilitary brainwashing of school children. At one rally, two trucks of boys paraded past onlookers. One carried boys holding baseball bats. It was decorated with German and French flags and displayed a sign saying, "Boys are boys in Germany and France." The other truck bore a banner reading, "Boys are now soldiers in New York State." Young boys with rifles hung over the sides.[11]

War supporters also held demonstrations. In May, 100,000 soldiers and civilians marched in a Preparedness Parade. Women's peace advocates appeared to distribute pamphlets that opposed the parade. The women hung a banner opposite the reviewing stand that asked:

> *There are only 100,000 of you. You are not the only patriots. 200,000 farmers, 500,000 mine workers and organized labor of America are opposed to what you and Wall St. are marching for. Are you sure you are right?"*[12]

New York women organized an art exhibit titled War Against War. This was the beginning of many mass artistic expressions against war by women painters, sculptors, novel-

ists, and playwrights. The exhibit was so successful that it had 7,000 viewers within a few days. The exhibit traveled to various sites in New York State and to Boston and Chicago.

Some women peace builders, including social workers Jane Addams and Crystal Eastman, sought stronger action. As the country prepared for war, they launched the American Union Against Militarism. The union held huge rallies in most major cities to encourage citizens to refuse war preparations. The union's most extreme stand was its firm opposition to drafting men as soldiers. Instead, it urged a passive, nonviolent national defense.

On February 14, 1917, Congress dealt a severe blow to

war protesters. The Espionage Act permitted the president to restrict the press and mail. He could claim that anyone who held meetings against the draft was disloyal to the government and have them jailed. The law was directed at citizens in sympathy with Germany, but it gave government officials a weapon to silence dissent and create fear of Germany.

The Espionage Act, coupled with the Sedition Act of 1918, seriously crippled women's war protests. Women received fines and jail sentences for antiwar speeches or writings. The number of rallies decreased, and the Woman's Peace Party newsletter, *Four Lights*, went out of business after Justice Department investigations. In a last gasp, author Katherine Anthony wrote "The Sister Susie Peril," a scathing article condemning women who choose relief work to be patriotic.

By April 2, President Wilson requested a declaration of war. Jeannette Rankin, the first congresswoman and a loyal pacifist, voted with 49 other representatives against the war, stating: "I want to stand by my country, but I cannot vote for war. I vote no."[13] The vote passed, and the country prepared to fight.

During the war, some women again assumed jobs left by soldiers, while others joined war relief projects. Woman's Peace Party leaders split in their support of the war. Carrie Chapman Catt was a pacifist but declared a patriotic duty to back the government. She even pledged her National American Woman Suffrage Association (NAWSA) to support relief efforts, hoping that a display of patriotism would help bring women the vote. The NAWSA bulletin, the *Woman Citizen*, ran recipes for meals without staples—such as meat, wheat, and butter—that were in short supply during the war. Soon after, the Woman's Peace Party canceled Catt's membership.

The Woman's Peace Party lost momentum and members to the belief that U.S. involvement in World War I was necesssary. Some members followed NAWSA's lead and joined war relief efforts. They acted on their strong convictions that if women gained the vote they could regain peace. Women such as militant suffragist Alice Stone believed that nothing—not even war—should deter women from seeking the vote. Her followers mounted a steady stream of rallies, pickets, and petitions for women's suffrage. Other party members maintained pacifist views, despite growing enthusiasm for war. While Catt's women knit socks for soldiers and wore shorter skirts to conserve material, women like Addams visited battlefields and reported the devastation. Most embattled peace activists tried to look beyond the war to a peace settlement free of blame.

## AFTER THE WAR

Pacifists managed to maintain the Woman's Peace Party as a loosely run organization until the war ended on November 11, 1918. Immediately, Jane Addams and Dr. Alice Hamilton traveled to Germany to help local Quakers, YWCAs (Young Women's Christian Association), and Red Cross chapters organize food programs. Then efforts shifted to assembling the next International Congress, one that would embrace the Central Powers.

From May 12 to May 17, 1919, Zurich peace seekers hosted a gathering of 211 women from around the world. The meeting included National Association of Colored Women founder Mary Church Terrell. Addams made a special attempt to enlist nonwhite Woman's Peace Party members. She hoped to reverse racist stands that suffragists took to gain support from southerners for the woman's vote.

Terrell later remembered the meeting: "Since I was the only delegate who gave any color to the occasion at all, it finally dawned on me that I was representing the women of all nonwhite countries in the world."[14]

Congress women protested the Treaty of Versailles and its formation of the League of Nations, a court of international cooperation. The women agreed with the idea behind the league, but American women were disappointed with terms of the treaty. They believed that keeping

Germany out of the league, plus imposing a food blockade and large payments for war damages on the Central Powers, only deepened Germany's resentment from losing the war. Such punishment, they pointed out, surely invited future revenge.

The women asserted that league membership must be open to all nations. Further, they maintained that women should have a place in the peace process. They demanded that a "Women's Charter" be added to the peace treaty to advance equal rights for the world's citizens, especially women and minorities.

At the close of the meeting, delegates agreed to resume their international women's organization as a way to "further peace, internationalism, and the freedom of women,"[15] With new resolve, the congress reorganized into the Women's International League for Peace and Freedom (WILPF), an organization that continues to this day. Jane Addams became the WILPF president and Emily Greene Balch the secretary-treasurer. Their leadership established a strong U.S. influence.

The international WILPF headquarters moved into the two-story Maison Internationale in Geneva, Switzerland, to outline the path to a more peaceful world. Similarly, the U.S. branch of WILPF opened its headquarters in Washington, D.C. The WILPF became the first nonviolent group to lobby legislators for peaceful foreign policies and social change for women and children.

# PICKING UP THE PIECES FROM WAR

# 7

*This is the time for us to work fast, not when the war comes.*

—Jessie Wallace Hughan,
  founder of War Resisters League, 1923[1]

A fter the war, women in several European countries gained the vote. Carrie Chapman Catt led two million U.S. suffragists to victory in 1920 with the ratification of the Nineteenth Amendment. The amendment granted suffrage to 35 million women who had never voted before in a public election. Women's suffrage also doubled African-American voting power. Hopes were high for women's political clout and permanent peace.

But women failed to unite into a solid voting bloc, as hoped and feared. Overall voting decreased throughout the 1920s and 1930s as women and men grew disenchanted with politics. Many African Americans, men and women, faced violence and local laws designed to keep them from voting. White men continued to wield the nation's real decision-making power. Women peace seekers realized that more than suffrage was needed for true equality and lasting peace.

The women's movement in general steadily lost workers after gaining the vote. Many suffrage activists returned to projects in familiar settings within the home, school, community, and church. Still, these women retained the powerful sense of what can be accomplished by joining together to advance a cause. Although few women achieved entry into the male political machine, most suffragists remained active outside the home. Women continued to influence major reforms in workers' rights, education, health care, housing, street sanitation, and child protection. Gaining a nonviolent world seemed as important as ever.

World War I had exacted a terrible toll. Modern weapons and warfare with "tanks, automatic machine guns, airplanes, and poison gases"[2] raised civilian and military losses to new heights. Ten million soldiers died, with 116,516 deaths from the United States alone. Families were shattered, and the economy was in turmoil. Even though the Allies won, many American women wondered whether war was worth the cost.

## REDEFINING WOMEN'S PEACEWORK

Hundreds of mixed-gender peace groups sprang up following the war, and many women joined. Yet the general feeling among peace builders, especially suffragists, was that women needed to create their own power structure. Outspoken lawyer Madeline Doty said in 1924, "We will never build up a strong group of women, capable of doing effective things, if we let men lecture to us and then adopt what they say."[3]

Well-known suffrage leaders, such as Carrie Chapman Catt, agreed that women should pursue peace independently. Catt contended that men were incapable of remaining nonviolent. In 1921, she insisted that "war is in the blood of men; they can't help it. They have been fighting ever since the days of the cavemen. There is a sort of honor about it."[4]

Old divisions within the WILPF resulted in the rise of four main U.S. women's peace groups during the 1920s.

The groups united for major campaigns but usually followed their own agendas.

The first split came in 1919 when Fanny Garrison Villard resigned from the WILPF to form the Women's Peace Society (WPS). Villard wanted a strict pacifist peace group. Peace Society members rejected WILPF support of the League of Nations because the league backed a watchdog army.

In a bold move, the Women's Peace Society required members to sign a pledge against war. The society's platform promoted complete disarmament and free trade. Moreover, members absolutely opposed any money or relief work going for armed forces, even for the country's defense. The society combined educational campaigns with lobbying in Washington to advance its platform.

Villard's financial control kept the group alive even though it was one of the smallest women's peace groups. The Women's Peace Society reached only 1,600 members, mostly in New York State and Washington, D.C. Villard died in 1928, and the group sputtered to an end by 1933.

Christine Ross Barker, a Canadian WILPF member, admired the Peace Society's extreme pacifist philosophy. Barker wrote to the Women's Peace Society and proposed a joint conference between women peace workers in Canada, Latin America, and the United States. From August 19 to August 21, 1921, pacifist women met to form the Women's Peace Union of the Western Hemisphere. Thereafter, each country's branch of the union established its own means of preventing war.

In the United States, another peace group, the Women's Peace Union, required a pledge from its members similar to the Women's Peace Society vow. Union members Elinor Byrns and Caroline Lexow drafted a proposed amendment to the U.S. Constitution that would have made war illegal. The problem was finding someone in Congress willing to back the amendment. North Dakota senator Lynn Joseph Frazier finally agreed to introduce the bill in 1926. Frazier unsuccessfully presented a version of the same amendment to each Congress until 1939. The next year the Women's Peace Union disbanded.

By 1924, Catt was ready to redirect her suffrage energies toward an earlier concern—world peace. Yet she still smarted from losing her Women's Peace Party membership for supporting war relief in favor of women's suffrage. Catt planned to form her own group with a different strategy from the others, one that blended her successful organizing and training skills.

Catt united the largest and most powerful women's associations into the National Committee on the Cause and Cure of War (NCCCW). This umbrella group supported lasting world peace without addressing issues deemed antigovernment or controversial. Catt's traditional, non-threatening stand attracted 11 national social, charity, professional, and reform groups. Together they sponsored educational programs and state and national conferences.

Catt's goal was to keep communication among these groups open. Therefore, she only focused on their policies that involved peace. By avoiding conflict, the NCCCW gained widespread support from government and women nationwide. Within 10 years, the NCCCW influenced national women's groups representing more than five million members. By 1934, almost 20 percent of the U.S. adult population was concerned with peace.

Throughout the 1920s and 1930s, women's groups kept the cause of peace alive through study groups, pamphlets, lobbying—anything to remind the public about the madness of World War I. In one of many bold moves, the WILPF hired pilot Ruth Nichols to drop leaflets on the 1931 Chicago Democratic party convention. The Women's Peace Society distributed flyers in department stores to protest the sale of war toys. The Parent-Teacher Association, which keeps quiet during most debates today, pushed for programs to teach school children how to prevent war. Peace seekers held street demonstrations with songs, candlelight ceremonies, and prayer vigils.

After making a record-breaking cross-country trip in 1930, aviator Ruth Nichols is welcomed to New York by her mother. The WILPF hired Nichols to drop leaflets on the 1931 Chicago Democratic party convention.

English teacher and pacifist Dr. Jessie Wallace Hughan organized No More War parades down Wall Street, the center of New York City's high-powered business district. Between 1931 and 1934, the number of marchers grew from 300 to more than 20,000. Hughan also urged young men to renounce war at annual Armistice (now Veterans) Day rallies on college campuses. Parade petitions warned: "Let us now in this great Peace Demonstration, join with many thousands in a crusade for a warless world. Another year may be too late. This is the hour!"[5]

On the surface, peace groups secured some important gains. In 1928, National Committee on the Cause and Cure of War member groups held 14,000 meetings to recommend international support of the Kellogg-Briand Pact. Any nation that signed agreed to hold discussions before proclaiming war.

As a result of NCCCW and WILPF prodding, 62 nations endorsed the treaty. The same year, the Senate confirmed U.S. agreement to the pact by a vote of 85 to 1. One drawback was that the agreement never questioned a country's right to defend itself. The military could still prepare for war by merely claiming the country was in danger.

Another major breakthrough came after the WILPF called for congressional investigation of the arms industry. In 1934, WILPF lobbyist and peace leader Dorothy Detzer convinced North Dakota senator Gerald Nye, Senate Munitions Committee chair, to present a bill for funding committee hearings. The Senate allotted $15,000 to interview witnesses about government dealings with the arms industry during World War I. Members of the Women's Peace Union and WILPF participated in the hearings.

The Nye Committee discovered that companies earned excessive profits from wartime arms sales. Furthermore, the committee charged arms manufacturers with bribing public officials to vote for war in 1917. Their report revealed how industry leaders had influenced higher military funding and price fixing. The public was outraged.

## PEACE WOMEN AS SPIES

Women's peace group successes resulted in severe government backlash. Once again, peace workers came under ruthless attacks from government, big business, and hate groups, such as the Ku Klux Klan. Government agents spied on women's peace group meetings. The War Department (the present-day Department of Defense) reopened files on many reform leaders, including Jane Addams, Emily Balch, and Carrie Chapman Catt.

In 1921, the League of Nations held its first Geneva meeting. The same year, the U.S. Department of Justice launched its harsh "Red Hunt." The 1917 communist revolution in Russia triggered fears that communism and its state control of all wealth would spread. Italy's fear of communism paved the way for Fascist dictator Benito Mussolini. In Germany, it opened doors for the rise of Adolf Hitler. In the United States, anyone opposed to war and the military and for improving conditions for the poor was labeled a communist traitor, someone who wanted to overthrow the government.

Newspapers discredited peace women and their groups as spies. The worst charges came from the War Department in a 1923 document called the Spider Web Chart. The chart diagrammed links between women reformers, their organizations, and an international communist plot to damage U.S. security. Department librarian Lucia Maxwell distributed the chart with a mocking poem:

*Miss Bolshevik has come to town,*
*With a Russian cap and a German Gown,*
*in Women's clubs she's sure to be found,*
*For she's come to disarm AMERICA.*[6]

Government hate mongers dogged the women throughout the 1920s and early 1930s. Patriotic groups, such as the Daughters of the American Revolution, now distrusted their peaceful sisters and distanced themselves

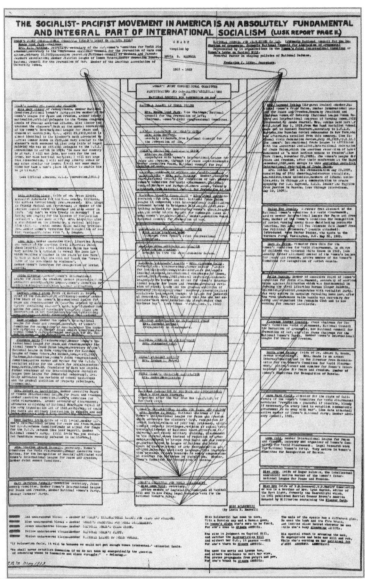

The Department of War's Spider Web Chart purported to show the myriad links between women reformers and an international communist plot to destroy the United States.

from peace organizations. Jane Addams received floods of hate mail labeling her an "enemy of the country." Her only crime was the strong belief that there was a better way to show love of country than by dying in battle.

Some peace leaders tried to defend themselves against public attacks. WILPF leader Emily Balch was fired from Wellesley College because of her peace activities during World War I. She asserted: "It [the backlash against women reformers] is evidently related to the fact that women have succeeded in carrying through certain reforms . . . and that they seem likely to effect other social advances."[7]

Carrie Chapman Catt reminded an audience that the same people who opposed women's rights were against peace: "The little group who seem to have got this entire country hoodooed on the question of peace . . . , and the very man who is preparing the publicity calling everybody Red who does anything for peace is the very man who called all the suffragists Reds."[8]

Despite criticism, the women's peace movement remained strong. Of the eight major U.S. peace groups, two were for women only: the WILPF and the National Committee on the Cause and Cure of War. Women constituted large memberships of the others, such as the Quaker-founded American Friends Service Committee.

Differences among these groups centered on their emphasis. Some, like the WILPF, sought to create international understanding through education programs. Others worked to influence U.S. foreign policy or pushed to curb the military.

Contacts between United States and international organizations made the promise of world peace seem possible. In 1932, government leaders planned the Geneva World Disarmament Conference. The National Committee on the Cause and Cure of War and WILPF gathered more than 600,000 signatures in the United States and 8 million worldwide to present at the conference. The same year the WILPF organized a Peace Caravan of 150 cars to carry the petitions from Hollywood, California, to President Herbert

Hoover in Washington, D.C., before the conference. Along the route, travelers staged rallies in 125 cities, grabbing front-page headlines and receiving formal backing from 56 mayors.[9]

Jane Addams, in 1931, and Emily Greene Balch, in 1946, finally received world recognition for their peace efforts with the Nobel Peace Prize. These two reform leaders were aging, however, as were other key women in peace organizations. Their dynamic leadership became difficult to replace. By the middle 1930s, membership in peace movements dwindled. Financial hardships caused by the Great Depression redirected women's energies closer to home. More women took jobs to help make ends meet. Movies, such as *The Front Page* (a 1940 version of this film would be entitled *His Girl Friday*), and radio soap operas, including "Hilda Hope, M.D.," glorified competent, single working women.

Nevertheless, women's peace groups continued to forge new pathways. They moved away from the assumption that as females and mothers it was women's duty to press for peace. Instead, they established a stronger connection between women's rights, social justice, and world peace.

To aid these causes, female peace workers brought local labor leaders and farmers together. The feeling was that working women had greater power to strike for change. This reasoning deepened after 900 African-American women walked out of St. Louis pecan factories in 1933. They were joined by white co-workers who agreed it was time to end discrimination. Factory owners "tried to divide the women, offering whites increased wages if they returned to work. The answer was returned by 1,500 women of both races marching on City Hall, and the proprietor gave in."[10]

Internationally, peace seekers opposed repressive governments in Europe. Many joined relief efforts for the Spanish Civil War. They worried about the alarming rise of tyranny in other nations and spoke out against racism and anti-Semitism at home.

These activities resulted in overwhelming support for

peace. A 1937 poll showed that 95 percent of the American people agreed that the U.S. should keep out of another war like World War I. But the climate abroad was already changing rapidly. In the end, nothing short of war could prevent the atrocities occurring in Europe.

# ENTER THE BOMB

# 8

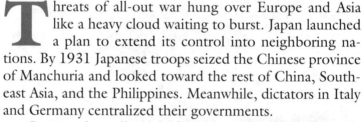

*There are other wars out there, Mother. They'll be worse. We haven't learned a thing!" She [mother] sighed. "May God have mercy upon us; we have none for one another.*

—from *High Hearts*, Rita Mae Brown[1]

**T**hreats of all-out war hung over Europe and Asia like a heavy cloud waiting to burst. Japan launched a plan to extend its control into neighboring nations. By 1931 Japanese troops seized the Chinese province of Manchuria and looked toward the rest of China, Southeast Asia, and the Philippines. Meanwhile, dictators in Italy and Germany centralized their governments.

German chancellor Adolf Hitler terrorized German citizens because of their religion, race, disability, or sexual preference. In 1933, he built Germany's first concentration camp in Dachau, supposedly for political prisoners. Thereafter, he initiated a series of boycotts and laws against Jews that would eventually spread across much of Europe. The same year both Japan and Germany withdrew from the League of Nations, foretelling the sweeping misery ahead.

Women peace seekers sounded the first alarms about the serious threats overseas. Dorothy Day founded the Catholic Worker movement in 1933 to combine religion with pacifism and social reform. Day organized U.S. supporters to distribute food and clothes to the poor and house homeless people. Equally important, her group published the reform newspaper *Catholic Worker* to rally for social action and nonviolence. By 1936, the paper's circulation reached 150,000 readers.

Day repeatedly reported her concern over the growing German prejudice against Jews. She was appalled that the United States resisted moves to assist an oppressed group. President Franklin Roosevelt refused to reduce immigration barriers to allow Jews into the United States. Consequently, millions of men, women, and children were abandoned to Nazi cruelty. "America is big enough to find a refuge for persecuted Jews," Day asserted in speeches and articles.[2]

The WILPF recommended nonviolence and U.S. mediation of problems abroad. Members called for withdrawal of U.S. ambassadors from Japan. They urged that the Kellogg-Briand Pact outlawing war be imposed against Japan and Germany. In addition, they pushed for a League of Nations inquiry into how to contain these aggressive nations.

The WILPF sent groups overseas to foreign trouble spots to support European women working for peace. But Europe's WILPF branches already felt the heavy hand of harsh governments. Nazis raided the Munich WILPF office, destroying files and arresting women. In 1933, the Swiss government accused WILPF international secretary Camille Drevet of spreading extremist lies and ordered her from the country. Swiss authorities received a flood of protest from around the world and quickly dropped the charges. Still, these episodes were signs of trouble ahead.

Like many American women, Carrie Chapman Catt worried about the unequal struggles between neutral countries and armed hostile nations. Catt visited several countries to assist local women's groups. For her aid, Catt was awarded the esteemed White Rose of Finland. In 1935, the Turkish government issued a postage stamp in her honor.

## REACTIONS TO FOREIGN ATTACKS

As Germany, Japan, and Italy invaded other nations, differences intensified among U.S. women peace seekers. Serious questions arose about which stand to take concerning the inhumane treatment people received abroad. What was the best way to end the violence? Was armed force really necessary to end such insane cruelty? The women found no easy answers to their questions.

Dorothy Detzer, WILPF national secretary from 1924 until 1947, demanded absolute pacifism. She and many other female peace activists led the campaign for total disarmament. Detzer insisted, "as pacifists, we can never yield our inalienable right to affirm and declare that war between nations or classes or races cannot permanently settle conflicts or heal the wounds that brought them into being."[3]

Various pacifist factions split from the WILPF and reorganized as new groups, such as the Keep America Out of War Congress and the People's Mandate to Governments to End War. Their members collected petitions calling for peace from world leaders. Some raised money for peace delegations to foreign countries. Pacifists advocated negotiation, oil embargoes, and product bans as ways to restrain Italy, Germany, and Japan.

Other women countered that force was sometimes necessary to end the spread of wrongdoing. And certainly the appalling events in Europe warranted drastic action. WILPF leaders, such as Emily Greene Balch, thought the American neutral policy showed indifference for people just because they lived elsewhere. Dr. Alice Hamilton, workplace hygiene pioneer, agreed that "it is not enough to . . . put out the fire when your own house is burning, and disinterest yourself . . . when the frame house next door is in flames and the children calling from its nursery windows to be taken out."[4]

On September 1, 1939, Germany invaded Poland, ending any hopes of a nonviolent solution. Two days later France and Great Britain officially declared war against Germany.

Communication between American and European peacemakers became more dangerous. International WILPF leader Gertrude Baer barely escaped from Germany in time. For safety, she moved to Princeton, New Jersey. Her main job there was to observe and report on the activities of the League of Nations' Economic Council. From her new office, Baer distributed WILPF quarterly newsletters, which helped maintain limited wartime contacts among peace activists worldwide. Other peace workers were less fortunate, however. Many died in German concentration camps.

Peace groups from countries facing war redirected their energies toward civilian war relief and blocking the Germans. Danish women, for example, sold tiny white peace flags to protest the war. After Germany invaded Denmark in April 1940, women continued to sell the flags. Even some German soldiers wore them secretly under their lapels.

Once the German army occupied a country, formal women's peace groups usually dissolved. Thereafter, underground resistance networks secretly plotted against the Nazis. Members devised creative ways to save Jews and other citizens who were in danger. Former Polish WILPF members once snatched Jewish children from trains headed for death camps. Women in other occupied countries hid children and adults who were hunted by Nazis. Christians in Great Britain, Denmark, and Holland accepted Jewish children into their families and boarding schools.

Discovery of each brave deed meant deadly consequences for everyone involved. Yet many women and men acted bravely to save lives. Danish WILPF worker Rigmore Risberg Thomsen remembered:

*We couldn't work regularly because we had Gestapo [German police] in our [WILPF] office sometimes and the vice-chair was imprisoned at times. . . . [O]ne month before the German troops arrived, we succeeded in getting three hundred Jewish children out of Vienna and had them brought to Denmark. . . . [A]fter the German soldiers came, we had to help*

*most of them escape to Sweden. We also helped the Danish Jews to escape once the persecution really set in.*[5]

When Japanese planes bombed the U.S. naval base at Pearl Harbor, Hawaii, on December 7, 1941, the U.S.

peace movement came to a screeching halt. Now 96 percent of U.S. citizens polled wanted Congress to declare war against Japan. Congresswoman Jeannette Rankin, still a strong peace advocate, cast the single vote against war. She was the only representative to vote against U.S. involvement in both World War I and World War II.

Three days later Germany and Italy, backed by Japan, declared war against the United States. Ultimately, 59 countries participated in this global conflict. Even faithful pacifists approved of fighting to prevent America's destruction. Rather than openly support fighting, pacifists looked toward renewed peace efforts when World War II ended. Pacifists consoled themselves by supporting President Roosevelt's 1942 plan for the United Nations, an international coalition to replace the weak League of Nations.

## WORLD WAR II

As with earlier wars, World War II brought masses of women out of the home. Society's disapproval of a married woman working disappeared. Policy makers insisted that all women had a patriotic duty to keep the economy alive while their men fought. Once again, women filled jobs left by men in industry and the armed forces, and they discovered that they were quite capable of doing so-called "men's work."

Scores of higher-paying jobs suddenly opened to women as factories converted to war manufacturing. The aircraft industry alone hired 300,000 women drafters, welders, and machinists. Women who had averaged $24 a week in laundry, clerical, and food-service jobs now earned $40 a week assembling ships, airplanes, and guns. Posters of "Rosie the Riveter," a woman in overalls and bandanna, became the national symbol for women who supported their country by working in a defense plant.[6]

The war brought about striking changes for minority women. Thousands of Native American women and men left reservations for the first time. Almost 800 Native

American women enlisted in the military, and 1,200 accepted war jobs. Women who remained on reservations assumed leadership roles abandoned by men who had joined the army or gone to work outside the reservation.

Traditional gender and race roles eased after Native American women took jobs alongside white sisters in city factories. Tribal boundaries faded as members from different nations met and organized. By the end of the war, Native American women questioned their support of a war overseas for freedoms that they never received from the U.S. government.

African-Americans wondered the same thing. They worked and fought for their country, yet they continued to face segregation, violence, low wages, and poor living conditions at home. Many black women moved to cities seeking the same wartime opportunities as other women. Instead, they received the most dangerous, menial, and low-paying jobs. During the 1940s, isolated groups of black women led boycotts, much like those promoted by Ida B. Wells. Their slogan was "Don't Buy Where You Can't Work."[7]

More than 350,000 women enlisted in armed forces, mainly replacing men in home-front duties. But the Navy's WAVES (Women Appointed for Voluntary Emergency Services) excluded African-American women until 1944. Other female armed forces isolated blacks in separate units, a practice that continued until the 1950s. A black army nurse suffered a beating and jail term just because she dared to board an Alabama bus before white passengers.

Even educated women experienced Jim Crow, the system of racial segregation. In 1941, Howard Law School student Pauli Murray wrote of the double prejudice she faced as a woman and black, even in an African-American school. "Howard Law School equipped me for effective struggle against Jim Crow. . . . [I]t was also the place where I first became conscious of the twin evil of discriminatory sex bias, which I quickly labeled Jane Crow."[8]

IN APRIL 1943, WAVES DO CALISTHENICS AT A U.S. NAVAL TRAINING SCHOOL. DURING WORLD WAR II, MORE THAN 350,000 WOMEN ENLISTED IN THE ARMED FORCES.

The connection between the fight for racial equality at home and abroad was shameful. African-American women joined the National Association for the Advancement of Colored People (NAACP) and the recently formed Congress of Racial Equality (CORE), for all races, in larger numbers. They began to speak out about segregation in the military and defense industries. "We ought to throw fifty thousand Negroes around the White House, bring them from all over the country . . . until we get some action from the White House," declared a woman delegate at the 1940 Chicago civil rights convention.[9]

News of a plan for a mass African-American protest

march in the nation's capital prompted President Roosevelt to prepare an executive order that forbade hiring discrimination by defense contractors. The resulting Committee on Fair Employment Practices opened some job opportunities to women of color. Roosevelt assumed his order smothered any risk of racial fires. Yet sparks of a civil rights movement still smoldered, only to erupt 10 years later.

Women peacebuilders did what they could to ease problems from war. In 1943, women from varied peace groups organized the National Committee to Oppose Conscription of Women. The committee successfully blocked a bill to draft women into the civilian labor force. Until 1947, the group opposed any draft.

Pacifists continued to defend conscientious objectors. During World War II, the law required those who refused to fight to serve the country in another manner. Draft boards assigned conscientious objectors to noncombat military posts or civilian public service camps. Government camps were administered by the three main peace churches—American Friends Service Committee, Mennonites, and Church of the Brethren. About 75,000 men out of the 13 million drafted were conscientious objectors. Of these, 6,000 went to jail rather than have any part in fighting, and 12,000 went into service camps.

Dorothy Day wrote moving articles titled "Catholics Can Be Conscientious Objectors," "The Gospel of Peace," and "The Weapons of the Spirit" in the *Catholic Worker*. Jessie Wallace Hughan opposed putting men who refused armed service into work camps. She fought their laboring without pay and pushed for fair wages. Hughan, Day, and other pacifist women voiced concern about the brutal treatment noncombat men received in jails. Hughan also wrote the booklet "If We Should Be Invaded," offering nonviolent methods of resistance in case of foreign invasion.

Unable to stop the madness overseas, the WILPF focused on issues of racial injustice at home. Americans of Japanese descent had been unjustly relocated to internment camps after Japan attacked Pearl Harbor. Thousands of

Japanese-American citizens lost their homes, businesses, and civil rights because of unreasonable fear and racial discrimination. The WILPF and women peace workers in the American Friends Service Committee assisted Japanese-American families with personal and business concerns.

## HOPE AND FEAR

In 1946, the United States exploded atomic bombs over two Japanese cities: Hiroshima (August 6) and Nagasaki (August 9). Never before had a weapon of such destructive force been deployed. A single bomb from a plane over Hiroshima resulted in 100,000 civilian deaths. The two bombings motivated Japan to surrender immediately and brought the war to an end. The threat of worldwide destruction from this horrendous weapon, however, unleashed new concerns for peace seekers—some that remain today.

The aftermath of war brought renewed efforts to secure future world peace. But the only women's peace group to survive, the Women's International League for Peace and Freedom, was shaken to its core. Sixty WILPF branches had discontinued, and the prewar high of 14,000 members shrunk to 4,708. European branches struggled as women mourned dead members and destruction of their cities and towns.

Nevertheless, 200 WILPF members from 15 countries traveled to Luxembourg in August 1946. The war-weary women reflected on their peace work in the face of vast despair. Of the 64.8 million soldiers who fought in World War II, almost 15 million died and another 26.5 million lay wounded. The United States alone lost 54,246 lives and spent $67.4 billion in the war effort, even though the fighting never reached American soil. The women decided it was worth reviving the WILPF to ensure the world never experienced such horrors again.

For WILPF leaders, an important aspect of postwar peace involved supporting the United Nations (UN).

Unlike the bygone League of Nations, the UN promised real hope for settling international quarrels peacefully. WILPF leaders from the United States attended UN planning meetings in San Francisco. The WILPF relocated its office near the United Nations in New York City to monitor its programs. Members funded radio spots and educated the public about disarmament, child welfare issues, and freedom the world over.

Dorothy Detzer, outgoing WILPF president, was one of the first women to sound the alarm about the threat of nuclear war. "The atomic bomb fell not only on Hiroshima and Nagasaki but, in a psychological sense, on all of us," she announced in a report.[10]

Most WILPF members saw value in nuclear power for peaceful uses. Yet a few women besides Detzer understood the greater threat that atomic bombs brought into everyone's home. They saw the devastation the bombs had brought on Japan. Its economy nearly stopped. Bombs injured thousands more people than those who died instantly. Fifty percent of Japan's cities were wasted by American bombs. On one WILPF radio spot, the announcer insisted "a bomb doesn't care in the least whether you are wearing a soldier's uniform or a housewife's apron." In 1945, the WILPF published a pamphlet called "The Atomic Bomb and Its Message to You" to alert governments to "Make Peace or Perish."[11]

Divisions that had torn apart the WILPF before the war refused to heal. In 1948, many members opposed the North Atlantic Treaty Organization (NATO), an alliance of 12 nations with combined armed forces. They viewed any military pact as divisive to world unity. Others viewed the union as necessary to check any future aggression.

The reduced WILPF membership remained mostly older and middle-class. Many peacemakers bristled at the WILPF's guarded approach. They sought to connect women's rights, social justice, and world peace as suffragists had during the early twentieth century. Most postwar women peace activists embraced a more militant pacifism, one that actively sought peacemakers from every economic and minority group.

On November 26, 1945, women from the wartime French Resistance hosted a meeting of more than 800 women from 41 countries. From this world conference came the Women's International Democratic Federation, an organization of 81 million women, and its U.S. branch, the Congress of American Women (CAW). The U.S. division attracted a wide variety of women who fought injustices at every level of society. There were "housewives, working women, trade unionists, farmers, doctors, lawyers, artists and women in government."[12]

This new coalition of women rekindled the fighting spirit of the 1920s. The CAW stressed women's relationship to famous suffragists Susan B. Anthony and Elizabeth Cady Stanton and abolitionists Sojourner Truth and Harriet Tubman. Descendants of Anthony and Stanton were prominent members.

The CAW emphasized women's right to a just world. Its agenda included better employment opportunities and health care and a women's equal rights amendment. The CAW's daring international policies endorsed interaction between all nations, which reflected a strong multiracial agenda. This link between women's militant past and inclusive spirit renewed women's drive for peace. By 1949, the CAW attracted 250,000 members. Problems developed, however, when the CAW defended communism and the Soviet Union as key to the struggle for peace. Postwar America was too fearful of communism spreading and women gaining true equality for the CAW to last long.

# BEWARE THE BOMB

# 9

*We the people of the United Nations, determined to reaffirm faith in fundamental human rights, in the dignity and worth of the human person, in the equal rights of men and women and of nations large and small."[1]*

—Preamble to the UN Charter

T he postwar climate for independent women and peace seekers was grim. Most women became caught up in building new lives after years of economic depression and war. Public interests centered on the returning soldiers who had risked their lives for the country. The media now claimed that the least women could do was give these men their prewar jobs and return home as good wives and mothers. Freedoms that women had achieved during the war ended almost as abruptly as they had begun. Working women lost challenging, high-paying jobs in industry and manufacturing.

Still, many women—married and single—intended to keep working. Most of the three million women who left wartime jobs entered more traditional female occupations as secretaries, teachers, nurses, clerks, and social and service workers. Some only found part-time employment. As a result, women's average weekly pay dropped from $50 to $37.

Media and government pounded home the message

that women of all backgrounds belonged in the home. Magazines and newspapers replaced "Rosie the Riveter" with advertisements of women in heels and shirtwaist dresses caring for children, husbands, clothing, and appliances. Advertisements glorified happy women displaying the whitest shirts and shiniest dishes while preserving long fingernails, soft skin, and wrinkle-free aprons.

Dr. Benjamin Spock sealed women's fate by writing *Common Sense Book of Baby and Child Care*. The book hailed mothers as the best and only people to lovingly tend their preschool offspring. Women were told they were bad parents if they didn't make family their only profession. A 1950 *Atlantic Monthly* article by Agnes Meyer declared, "Women must boldly announce that no job is more exacting, more necessary, or more rewarding than that of housewife and mother."[2]

Postwar attitudes took their toll on women's peace building. Couples throughout the 1950s married earlier, divorced less, and produced more babies than during the war years. These trends kept women home, isolated from their equal rights as full citizens, and quiet about the inequities they and others endured. Most younger women were too busy with families to consider peace work.

Peace activities that did occur centered on women's primary role as good mother. Women protested civil defense drills in elementary schools and military training for boys in high school. Some peace workers joined groups with names such as WOMAN, World Organization of Mothers of All Nations. Anything associated with better mothering provided possible avenues for women peace activists to pursue.

## Spy Madness

The political climate in the United States was just as restrained. Past anxieties about communism had eased during the war when the Soviet Union and United States cooperated to battle Germany and Japan. But tensions never totally disappeared. The postwar peace bargain allowed

Soviets to split Eastern Europe from noncommunist countries, dividing Europe for the next 40 years. After the United States dropped the atomic bomb, mutual distrust dominated foreign policy. The Cold War, the undercurrent of unspoken conflict, descended over the superpowers.

From 1945 to 1949 the United States claimed a monopoly on atomic weapons. Then the Soviet Union tested its first atomic bomb in August 1949. The same year China installed a communist-backed government. The international balance of power shifted, and the arms race surged forward between east and west.

Greater fears of communists taking over the United States and the world reemerged. Military troops went wherever the United States believed intervention was in the country's best interest to contain communism. Anyone against war, bombs, and injustice was under suspicion of being procommunist and un-American. The U.S. government investigated members of the WILPF, the Congress of American Women, labor unions, media, and colleges. No one was exempt. Even Quaker women feeding starving children in Germany were suspect. In 1947, President Harry Truman questioned the loyalty of more than three million federal employees alone.

Spy madness escalated at an alarming rate after Senator Joseph McCarthy took over government inquiries. McCarthy launched an endless series of hearings before the House Un-American Activities Committee (HUAC). Those branded a "security risk" after testifying lost their job, freedom to travel overseas, and rights to move anywhere freely.

The committee expected citizens to reveal names of coworkers and friends they thought were communists. Those who courageously refused to cooperate were jailed. Committee charges ruined thousands of careers and lives.

Moreover, McCarthyism bred distrust that poisoned many long-standing women's groups. The WILPF leadership weakened as members withdrew because of unfounded fears that co-workers were dreaded communists. The Congress of American Women suffered the greatest assaults.

The Justice Department required the group to register as an enemy agent because it supported any peaceful teachings, including communism. A legal battle was the only way to continue, but success seemed doomed in the present political climate.

When the CAW dissolved in 1950, women lost a major voice for equal rights. No other existing group so closely connected women's concern for social and gender equality with world peace. Smaller women's groups and branches of the WILPF continued to work with the United Nations and protest the Korean War (1950–53), arms buildup, military draft, and troops in Haiti, Guatemala, and other Latin American countries. Yet McCarthyism stifled the growth of any widespread U.S. women's peace movement until the early 1960s.

Meanwhile, the arms race continued unchecked. By 1960, the earth had absorbed 190 atom and hydrogen bomb tests. Of these, 125 were conducted by the United States, 44 by the Soviet Union, and 21 by the United Kingdom. Radiation levels in the atmosphere rose sharply from frequent nuclear explosions.

Scientists soon discovered unsafe levels of strontium 90 in milk. *Consumer Reports* magazine warned: "The fact is that fresh milk, which looks and tastes just as it always had, nevertheless contains . . . an unseen . . . toxic substance known to accumulate in human bone."[3]

Shortly after the article appeared, President John Kennedy proposed an increased military budget. Soviet premier Nikita Khrushchev countered by constructing the Berlin Wall, splitting the city into East and West Berlin. Kennedy's response was to resume above-ground bomb tests, which had not occurred in three years.

Several male-run peace groups monitored the shaky foreign relations. Yet they seemed either too fearful of McCarthy or too indifferent to the looming world crisis to act. In 1961 Dagmar Wilson and a group of alarmed mothers met in Washington, D.C., to devise a plan to fight these threats to their children's safety. Their group, Women

Strike for Peace, first picketed the White House. One month later on November 1, they organized a one-day mass strike of 50,000 "housewives" in 60 cities.

Similar to the women in the Greek play *Lysistrata*, these wives and mothers left their homes and offices to demand peace. They marched by local city halls and federal government buildings, many pushing baby buggies. Only this time the women held picket signs that read "End the Arms Race, Not the Human Race" and "Stop Testing Now!" In Washington, D.C., a collie that joined about 800 women in front of the White House wore a bib saying, "Please No More Strontium 90."

Women Strike for Peace appealed to the public's view of females. The women embodied postwar ideals about women's duty to family and community. Members tended to be white, educated, and middle-class. White House marchers wore white gloves and flowered hats and were accompanied by their children. *Newsweek* commented that the strikers "were perfectly ordinary-looking women . . . like the women you would see driving ranch wagons, or shopping at the village market, or attending PTA meetings."[4]

Women Strike for Peace members rejected the formal structure and pacifist views of WILPF, although the two groups often worked together and membership overlapped. Instead, they took pride in spontaneous marches, petition drives, and demonstrations. Connected by telephone trees of interested friends, Women Strike for Peace mobilized members for conferences, letter-writing campaigns, and trips overseas to lobby hostile governments. Like their nineteenth-century foremothers, these peace seekers rediscovered they had talents beyond the home. Yet, few knew of the rich heritage that they inherited from earlier female peace builders.

Media and government found it harder to dismiss such respectable peace activists as crazies. Their simple message of being responsible mothers who wanted to protect life rallied a following against the military, government foreign policy, and the untouchable House Un-American Activities

Committee. Ladylike women joined by the thousands, often forming local branches with less-threatening names, such as Women for Peace.

Fears of foreign influence dogged Women Strike for Peace. Anticommunists were concerned that "the pro-Reds have moved in on our mothers and are using them for their own purpose."[5] In 1962, the HUAC subpoenaed Women Strike for Peace leaders. Unafraid of the committee's absurd charges, the women made a mockery of the congressmen.

Supporters carrying jabbering babies filled the committee room. The women gave flowers and bouquets to witnesses and applauded their performances.

Women Strike for Peace witness Blanche Posner scolded counsel Alfred Nittle:

> *You don't quite understand the nature of this movement. . . . [It] was inspired and motivated by mothers' love for their children. When they were putting their breakfast on the table, they saw not only wheaties and milk, but . . . strontium 90 and iodine 131. . . . If you gentlemen have children or grandchildren, you should be grateful to the Women Strike for Peace, or whatever peace movement is working to stop nuclear testing.[6]*

At a later session Nittle asked WSP cofounder Dagmar Wilson about communists in Women for Peace. Wilson answered confidently, "If only we could get them on our side."[7]

The press went wild. Headlines blared, "Peace Gals Make Red Hunters Look Silly" and "It's Ladies Day at the Capitol: Hoots, Howls and Charm." A cartoon appeared in newspapers showing two congressmen sitting at the HUAC table. One said to the other, "Which is un-American, women or peace?"

Using the language of motherhood, Women Strike for Peace exposed the feared committee for the sham it was. They made the logical questioning of war, government, and politics acceptable for the first time in decades. Their earliest success came with passage of the 1963 Test Ban Treaty between the United States and the Soviet Union. This victory fueled Women Strike for Peace members to press for an end to nuclear arms and greater global cooperation.

The WILPF sent delegations to visit women peace activists in China and the Soviet Union. Together peace women called for admitting the People's Republic of China into the United Nations. Women Strike for Peace members joined with WILPF to call for a ban on the manufacture, advertisement, and sale of war toys. These programs brought women out of their kitchens once again, paving the way for the next era of bolder female peace workers.

## PEACE WORK AT HOME

Few minority women had the luxury of sheltered suburban lifestyles. Racial segregation under the system of Jim Crow laws still kept southern African-American women from voting and earning a decent living. Black girls learned at a young age that they would never live in peace without equality and freedom from violence. Daring women renewed civil rights as a burning public issue.

Melba Pattillo Beals was only 15 when she protested the cruelties of segregation. She and eight other teenagers were the first students to integrate Central High School in Little Rock, Arkansas. Three years earlier, in 1954, the Supreme Court had decided the landmark *Brown vs. Board of Education* case, declaring segregation in public schools unconstitutional. Beals would battle angry mobs, telephone threats, acid-throwing attackers, and insults for the right to go to the same school as other children.

"While most teenage girls were listening to Buddy Holly's 'Peggy Sue,' watching Elvis gyrate, and collecting crinoline slips, I was escaping the hanging rope of a lynch mob, dodging lighted sticks of dynamite, and washing away burning acid sprayed into my eyes," remembered Beals.[8]

The nation received another major jolt from the budding civil rights movement after three women organized the Montgomery, Alabama, bus boycott. On December 1, 1955, Rosa Parks, an African-American seamstress and secretary for the National Association for the Advancement of Colored People (NAACP), sat in the black section of a bus after work. Riders quickly filled the white section of the bus, so the driver ordered Parks to give up her seat to a white passenger. Parks refused and was arrested.

Parks's lawyer said the law allowed her to go free. But Parks wanted to use the case to fight bus segregation in court, despite fears for her safety. Two other NAACP women, Jo Ann Robinson, a college-educated black woman, and Virginia Durr, a white activist for equality, backed her decision.

The women tapped into a network of women who already had planned a boycott. The women circulated thousands of fliers telling the African-American community that the time was right to boycott Montgomery buses. Four days after her arrest Parks was convicted. By then, no African-Americans rode city buses.

The boycott continued until Parks's successful appeal. To celebrate, more than 10,000 people marched to Montgomery's Holt Church. In the heat of the night, a young preacher named Rev. Martin Luther King Jr. pleaded for riders to continue the boycott and join him in other forms of nonviolent protest. King's speech established him as leader of nonviolent black resistance. Still, it was Parks and her grassroots women's network that launched the nationwide civil rights movement.

As in abolition days, women peace activists across the country emerged to support civil rights. But like their suffrage foremothers, women in the largely white peace groups grappled with how to deal with issues of black women. Some whites in Women Strike for Peace and WILPF opposed mixing peace and civil rights. Others emphasized that issues involving all women were welcome in their organization.

African-American women had their own view of peace. "If the next hundred years are going to be like the last, we don't care whether there is peace or not," one woman asserted.[9]

For many peace seekers, equal rights at home was as important as peace abroad. Women volunteered to leave their safe homes to register African-American voters in the South. Peace activist Joan Baez and other folk singers from around the country encouraged volunteers with their free-

dom songs. Fannie Lou Hamer, a poor black sharecropper turned civil rights leader, heard the message of equality in a church meeting in Ruleville, Mississippi. "I had never heard the freedom songs before. They really wanted to change the world I knew—they wanted Blacks to register to vote!"[10]

In 1965, 38 suburban Chicago white women rented a bus to attend a black-organized freedom march in Selma, Alabama. A violent confrontation on an Alabama bridge turned their bus around, but the women persisted. The next day they joined the march despite jeers and threats from angry whites along the way.

ON MARCH 16, 1965, ALICE HERZ SET FIRE TO HER
CLOTHING TO PROTEST THE ESCALATION OF U.S.
INVOLVEMENT IN THE VIETNAM WAR. IN A LETTER TO
HER DAUGHTER, HERZ WROTE, "I DO THIS NOT OUT
OF DESPAIR, BUT OUT OF HOPE." TEN DAYS LATER, SHE
DIED.

Peace artist Pearl Hirshfield recalled: "Civil rights marches generated First Amendment issues of the right to protest. Police and guards committed unlawful acts, but the pursuit of civil liberties bound people together. Anger overpowered our feelings of fear."[11]

Back in Evanston, Illinois, Hirshfield helped organize annual Peace and World Affairs backyard fairs. The fairs raised funds for peace abroad and civil rights in America. As opposition to government troops overseas heated, Hirshfield and other mothers gave out peace literature as well. Racist hate groups, like the White Circle League and Great Americans, telephoned threats to the women. "Peace was a dirty word back then," Hirshfield remembered.

Overriding other peace issues was the U.S. troop build-up in Vietnam. A string of presidents charged that communist North Vietnam was trying to seize South Vietnam. President Eisenhower initially sent military advisors in 1954 to support South Vietnam. By 1964, President Lyndon Johnson insisted that the fall of one Southeast Asian nation to communism meant the fall of others "like a row of dominoes." Following this reasoning, Johnson ordered the first military ground forces into battle.

On March 26, 1965, 82-year-old Alice Herz set herself on fire to protest U.S. involvement in Southeast Asia. Herz, a Michigan WILPF member and former German refugee, knew the horrors of war. She died within 10 days but left a note urging young people to fight against war.

Women's peace groups moved into high gear. The threat of full-scale war bolstered numbers in the two main women's peace organizations, the WILPF and Women Strike for Peace. Both united with other peace groups in an unprecedented display of antiwar demonstrations. Women opened draft-counseling centers in key cities to help conscientious objectors. They lobbied Congress and pushed to elect peaceful politicians, successfully launching WSP member Bella Abzug into Congress.

Jeannette Rankin, the congresswoman who voted against both world wars, challenged women to risk jail to stop the war. About 4,000 women answered her call for a 1969 Women Strike for Peace march on Washington, D.C. Eighty-eight-year-old Rankin and black civil rights leader Coretta Scott King led what became known as the Jeannette Rankin Brigade.

Catherine Stimson of Rutgers University recalls how Women Strike for Peace helped organize the brigade: "A coalition of women from the black civil rights movement, peace movement, and feminism, we took a train to Washington, D.C., on 15 January 1969. There, on a cold and snowy day, we marched through the streets of our capital, stamping our booted feet and exercising our First Amendment rights, calling on our country to stop the killing."[12]

The brigade broke new ground in outrageous acts. At another march to Arlington National Cemetery, marchers buried a dummy they called "Traditional Womanhood." An invitation to the "Burial of Traditional Womanhood" read:

> *Don't bring flowers. . . . Do be prepared to sacrifice your traditional female roles. You have refused to hanky-wave boys off to war. . . . And now you must resist . . . playing these same roles that are synonymous with powerlessness. . . . [W]e must learn to fight the warmongers on their own terms, though they believe us capable of only rolling bandages.[13]*

The onset of war awakened young people to the need for peace work, especially on college campuses. The average age of U.S. soldiers leaving for Vietnam was 18 years, compared with 24 years for World War II. Young women worried about losing friends and brothers, just as older women were anxious about their sons and husbands. Female students joined sit-ins at campus buildings and peaceful rallies and marches. As war dragged on, they helped burn draft cards and American flags.

President Richard Nixon's orders to bomb North Vietnam and invade nearby Cambodia unleashed a torrent of campus antiwar demonstrations. Protests were gaining so many antiwar backers that government moved to suppress dissent. On May 4, 1970, the Ohio National Guard shot 13 students at Kent State University, killing 4. One day later Mississippi police killed two Jackson State College students. Outraged students protested government control with a nationwide demonstration. One million students at more than 600 colleges, universities, and high schools boycotted class.

Newcomers to peace work soon discovered what suffragists had found earlier: men in civil rights and antiwar movements were unconcerned about fairness to women. Women protesters suffered beatings, jail, and now death alongside men. Yet women were refused leadership or decision-making positions. Many talented women who volunteered for the black Southern Christian Leadership Conference (SCLC) or antiwar Students for a Democratic Society (SDS) found themselves assigned to secretarial rather than leadership roles.

Ella Baker, head of the New York NAACP, had a rude awakening after receiving a junior position in SCLC. "As a woman, an older woman, in a group of ministers who are accustomed to having women largely as supporters, there was no place for me to come into a leadership role."[14]

Women of the 1950s accepted their behind-the-scenes fate. By the 1960s, however, more women followed the example set by the leaders of Women Strike for Peace. They demanded a greater voice in decisions affecting their lives and those of their children. They were willing to act on their own behalf and that of their family and country.

Many joined existing women's peace groups or formed their own. The older women of WILPF who saw themselves as peace builders rather than workers for women's rights held little appeal to free-spirited students. But Women Strike for Peace attracted hopeful war protesters who were also interested in expanding women's rights.

In 1966, Betty Friedan, author of the groundbreaking feminist book, *The Feminine Mystique*, helped found the National Organization of Women (NOW). The 30 original members sought to "bring American women into full participation in the mainstream of American society." This group gave new life to feminism, redefining it as "the idea that women were entitled to political, social, and economic equality with men."[15]

Motherhood was still an important theme for many peace seekers. Screenwriter Barbara Avedon's concern for peace deepened after her son was born. In 1967, Avedon united 15 friends into Another Mother for Peace. Within five years, the group amassed a mailing list of more than 250,000 people. Many famous stars of the day, including Donna Reed, who played the ideal mother in a television sitcom, lent their names.

Avedon's small group raised money for an Invest in Peace Fund by selling Mother's Day cards. In one year the group sold 200,000 cards. The money went to support legislators who voted against war. Each card read:

*For a Mothers' Day gift this year*
*I don't want candy or flowers.*
*I want an end to killing.*
*We who have given life*
*Must be dedicated to preserving it.*
*Please, talk peace!*[16]

In May 1969, Another Mother for Peace organized its first annual Mother's Day Assembly in Los Angeles. Artist Lorraine Schneider unveiled a logo of a large sunflower. Surrounding the flower were words shared by women peace seekers everywhere, "War is not healthy for children or other living things." The women went on to generate information about military buildup, chemical warfare, and nuclear effects on the environment. The group distributed a newsletter and peace materials until 1985.

Other peacemakers invented more extreme protests. In

1968, the New York WILPF picketed the annual Miss America contest in Atlanta. Women supposedly burned bras and handed out fliers headed "All Women Are Victims in This Man's War." This flier connected Vietnam and war with women's struggle for equal rights.

In March 1969, artist Yoko Ono and her musician husband John Lennon staged a "love-in" for peace. For one week the famous honeymoon couple received reporters in bed to call attention to world suffering and violence. Ono claimed, "We did a bed-in in Amsterdam . . . just to give people the idea that there are many ways to protest."[17]

A similar groundswell of peaceful protest came from youth across America. Nonviolent resistance to war in the 1960s and 1970s was expressed in such slogans as "Make Love Not War," "Power to the People" and "Peace, Love and Flower Children." The media labeled these young people the "me" generation because of their absorption in self-discovery. But they were really idealistic peacemakers who found their quest for free-spirited fun impossible as long as the threat of violence and nuclear destruction existed.

Women peace seekers of this era broadened the issue of peace. Peacekeeping expanded to saving individuals, the land, and the entire world for a better, hassle-free life. An important component of this struggle was saving the world from nuclear destruction.

# WOMEN HELPING WOMEN

*I was trying to empower women by showing them
that what they understood and the skills they built in
the community and family work they did were rele-
vant to making peace in the community at large
and dealing with social problems.*

—Elise Hansen Boulding in *Peacework*[1]

**M**assive protests against the Vietnam War slowly
won support in Washington, D.C. Before the
1972 election, President Richard Nixon opened
talks with North Vietnam. When these failed, Nixon ordered the cruelest bomb attacks of the war. Peace seekers
kept pushing for a peace settlement, arguing that economic
and human losses far outweighed any fear of communism.

When Nixon resigned in disgrace in 1973, many loyal
defenders of the war in Vietnam left Washington with him.
Congress voted to stop funds for the bombing of neighboring Cambodia, and troops were ordered to withdraw from
Vietnam. Two years later, North Vietnam destroyed the
South Vietnamese military, and any remaining U.S. military
advisors returned home.

Communism seemed to triumph but not before exacting an enormous toll on the United States and Vietnam.
The war cost the Vietnamese more than 2 million lives and
the destruction of countless villages. The United States
wasted more than $150 billion and 58,000 people. More-

over, government's policy of military violence to influence less powerful nations proved worthless. The United States lost its image abroad as a military power that never failed. At home, prowar politicians provoked tremendous distrust among citizens.

Yet lawmakers, in all their wisdom, persisted in sending troops around the globe to combat the spread of communism. Many conflicts involved smaller, poorer nations that had gained independence since World War II. Fifty new countries joined the United Nations during the early 1950s alone.

Civil war was common among these nations because of the political and economic chaos involved in establishing home rule. Power went to the wealthy few, leaving most people in poverty. U.S. corporations also exploited these nations for cheap labor and natural resources. Lawmakers feared that unrest left weaker countries open to communist takeover and pushed for military bases to protect U.S. investments.

Women peace seekers hoped U.S. political leaders had learned from the disastrous outcome of the Vietnam War. But with expanded military technology and U.S. soldiers stationed overseas, post-Vietnam threats to world safety seemed even greater. After prior wars, widespread women's peace activities decreased. With Vietnam, however, the spirit of nonviolence continued to thrive after troops came home.

## PEACE AND HUMAN RIGHTS

As the war revived women's interest in peace, the growing women's movement stressed the need for a new global order of mutual respect. Pacifist women believed that if they could create a world where everyone—men and women—received social, economic, and political justice, true peace would be possible.

Pacifist Barbara Deming connected peace and civil rights: "I think violence in our society is the attempt by men to claim women and children as their property. . . . We ARE one kind—women and men. And that [nonviolent] world IS possible."[2]

The United Nations declared 1975 as International Women's Year. Meetings during the year provided a forum to plan a peaceful agenda for women everywhere. The year proved so successful that the United Nations sponsored a Decade for Women. Established groups, such as the WILPF and Women Strike for Peace, played an important role in keeping the goal of a warless world alive. Throughout the decade they held local and global events.

Many younger women and women of color joined smaller, single-issue groups. Because the groups were sponsored by the UN, issues affecting nonwhite women received greater attention. Hearing stories about women from less-developed nations underscored the connection between international and domestic violence. Women peace activists realized that world tensions would continue unless countries guaranteed their citizens basic needs, such as food, shelter, health care, and jobs.

The women who gathered at UN conferences linked human rights at home and abroad. Some women had different opinions about how to end violence between and within countries. Yet most recognized that the road to peace was through world disarmament and redirecting arms money to help raise individuals from poverty.

United States peace builders agreed that increased military budgets drained the country of money better spent on social services. They were appalled that a two-week military budget equaled the annual cost of enough food, water, education, health, and housing for everyone in the world.[3] A New York WILPF pamphlet charged: "Women Demand Disarmament: 1975 Is International Women's Year—Military Spending Threatens the Goals of Equality, Development, Peace."[4]

The UN Decade for Women drew serious attention to peace concerns. Many women who had previously felt powerless to oppose violence joined peace actions during this

THE JAPANESE DELEGATION AWAITS THE OPENING CEREMONIES AT THE 1975 INTERNATIONAL WOMEN'S YEAR CONFERENCE IN MEXICO CITY.

promising era. Their appeal for peace went beyond the usual "for the good of the children." Now women fought to reject rigid gender roles that kept men and women from being kinder, gentler, and equal.

Energized peace builders included whites and non-whites, middle class and poor from developing and industrial nations. Earlier women peace seekers took great pains to appear tasteful and polite. Activists of the 1970s adopted more militant and creative tactics. The revived women's peace movement resounded with stirring songs, dramatics, writings, debates, and coalitions of women from varied walks of life. And their message extended to preserve all of nature—the people, air, water, and land.

In Minneapolis, a group called Women Against Military Madness (WAMM) tried to rekindle the spirit of protest from the Vietnam War. Members defended their all-women group: "All of society is victimized by rampant militarism. However, women lack access to the policy making levels of the three institutions which run the United States, the government, Pentagon, and corporations. Thus women are doubly victimized and can only liberate themselves."[5]

## BAN NUCLEAR WEAPONS

Throughout the 1970s, Australian-born pediatrician and antinuclear activist Helen Caldicott lectured nationwide to educate the public about the effects of radiation. In her talks, Caldicott warned that "blown from the west to east by stratospheric winds, these particles descend to the earth in rainfall and work their way through soil and water into the food chain, eventually posing a serious threat to human life."[6] Caldicott revived the dying Physicians for Social Responsibility, an anti–nuclear arms coalition of health care workers. She also wrote a searing attack against the nuclear industry in *Missile Envy and Nuclear Madness: What You Can Do.*

## WOMEN'S PENTAGON ACTION

A 1979 accident at the Three Mile Island nuclear power plant in Pennsylvania inflamed women's rage against the mounting arms race and threats to the environment. Nuclear energy benefited industrial giants and the military at the expense of air, water, and food. Furious East Coast women met to discuss what they could do to protest nuclear energy and testing. The women decided to march on the Pentagon, headquarters of the nation's military and "symbol of the all-male violence" they opposed.[7]

From this meeting came the Women's Pentagon Action, a leaderless group of women who opposed military spending and weapons expansion. In their 1980 Unity Statement, Women's Pentagon Action organizers demanded:

AT A 1983 PRESS CONFERENCE IN BOSTON, DR. HELEN CALDICOTT, ANTINUCLEAR ACTIVIST AND FORMER HEAD OF PHYSICIANS FOR SOCIAL RESPONSIBILITY, SPEAKS OUT AGAINST THE DEPLOYMENT OF NUCLEAR WEAPONS.

*We are gathering at the Pentagon on November 16 because we fear for our lives . . . the life of this planet, our Earth, and the life of the children who are our human future. . . . Their exploitation and the organized destruction of never to be seen again species threatens and sorrows us. . . . We want an end to the arms race. No more bombs. No more amazing inventions for death.*[8]

The actual 1980 Women's Pentagon Action unfolded in four stages. Each stage dramatized how the women felt about the Pentagon and their determination to challenge military decisions. Colorful 22-foot puppets and beating drums signaled entry into another theatrical stage.

During the first stage of mourning, 2,000 moaning marchers snaked through rows of tombstones at Arlington Cemetery. Upon reaching the Pentagon, mourners constructed their own cemetery on the front lawn. Each tombstone remembered a victim of violence from war, rape, radiation poisoning, government tyranny, or unsafe abortion.

After mourning came rage. Angry protesters chanted "Take the Toys Away from the Boys." Women shook their fists at Pentagon officials who peered through doorways and windows. At a signal, the demonstrators' rage turned to the third stage, empowerment. Two lines of women circled the Pentagon, singing peace songs. Marchers linked hands or ribbon and yarn woven with flowers, poems, and other gentle symbols.

The last stage was defiance, a final nonviolent action for peace. Women wove the Pentagon doors shut with yarn and blocked entry with their bodies. Police threatened the protesters and cut the yarn. But women quickly wove the threads again.

After an hour and several warnings, police arrested about 120 women. Those who pleaded guilty for blocking entrances received an unusually harsh 10 days in jail for a

Last fall over 2,000 women from thoughout the Northeast went to the Pentagon to demonstrate their mourning, rage, empowerment and defiance. About 150 women were arrested.

Photo by Dorothy Marder

*BECAUSE*, each day, the men in power are making decisions, appointments, laws that put the people of this country under attack; especially women, people of color, lesbian and gay people...

*BECAUSE*, each day, the men in power flaunt that power, pushing the world closer and closer to nuclear destruction...

*WE WOMEN MUST ACT*

# WOMEN RETURN TO THE PENTAGON
## November 15 & 16, 1981

For More Information, Contact:

**Women's Pentagon Action**
339 Lafayette St.
New York, NY 10012
212-254-4961

*The Women's Pentagon Action includes women from all over the Northeast. We come from many backgrounds and have many concerns—feminism, women's rights, peace, ecology, lesbian rights. Our understanding of the connections between these issues is expressed in the Unity Statement on the reverse side.*

Distributed by WAR RESISTERS LEAGUE

A LEAFLET ADVERTISES A 1981 WOMEN'S MARCH ON THE PENTAGON, THE HEADQUARTERS OF THE U.S. DEPARTMENT OF DEFENSE.

first offense and one month if they had been arrested before. The next year's Women's Pentagon Action drew nearly 3,000 women, with about 43 arrests.

One year later Ronald Reagan became president. For the next eight years he promoted nuclear expansion to rebuild America's lost military advantage. Distrust among the superpowers increased, escalating the arms race. By 1981, the United States convinced NATO countries that more missiles could protect Europe from nuclear war. That August, the United States stationed cruise missiles on air force bases throughout western Europe.

## Peace Camps

Nuclear dangers brought a new wave of women's peace actions. European and United States women drew courage from the Women's Pentagon Action. A group of women and men marched 125 miles from Cardiff to the Greenham Common outside London to protest placement of 96 cruise missiles in Britain. On September 5, 1980, women stayed to establish a lasting peace camp. They decided to make it a women-only settlement.

Campfires and multicolored plastic-covered tents mushroomed on public land surrounding the cruise missile base at Greenham Common. Women, some with children, came and went, while others stayed full-time. The original small group attracted more than 30,000 women over the next 14 years. Campers staged many peaceful protests, blocking military expeditions and weaving ribbons through the gates. The most destructive action the women took was to paint peace symbols on military vehicles.

Yet the camp brought a flood of protest from police, townspeople, and the world military establishment. Women suffered jail, hot pokers, soldier and media insults, property seizures, and maggots. Their backs ached from sleeping on mats, and the boredom seemed endless. Still, peace campers knew the misery was small compared with nuclear destruction.

Their goal was to heighten public awareness of nuclear weapons. The more opposition they received, the more they knew governments feared their presence would bring change. Indeed, Greenham inspired local British governments to declare more than 140 nuclear-free zones during the next six years.[9]

More than a hundred women's peace camps sprang up during the 1980s. The largest and longest-running camp in the United States formed after one million people marched for nuclear disarmament through New York City's Central Park on June 12, 1982. Women from WILPF and the Quaker-based American Friends Service Committee had already demonstrated at the Seneca Army Depot in upstate New York, storage site for Europe-bound missiles. Now they talked of founding a camp similar to Greenham to show unity with their British peace sisters.

The WILPF raised money for a nearby farm where the women could live safely. By July 1983, the Seneca Women's Encampment for a Future of Peace and Justice opened in the town of Romulus near the army depot. Because of its location, the camp had ties to important events in the history of women's activism: nearby Seneca Falls was the birthplace of the women's rights movement in 1848, and the region was the traditional home of the Iroquois, whose women had sought to end tribal fighting.

The Seneca camp attracted up to 3,000 women at one time. They came from varied races, professions, and opinions. Their common thread was a strong desire to make the world a better place to live. Once again, demonstrators connected equal rights and quality of life for women and men with peace.

Campers showed concern for peace and fair living in everyday activities. They emphasized how injustice to one woman affects the entire community and women everywhere. Seneca demonstrations explored the rich traditions that women shared. With the Washer Woman Action of 1983, they "acted out the daily washing, wringing, and hanging up of clothes . . . as a tribute to the work of the washer woman and all women's work."[10]

Peace builders in Palo Alto, California; Ann Arbor, Michigan; Tucson, Arizona; Savannah, Georgia; and Sperry, Minnesota, patterned camps after Seneca. Moreover, peace camps became a model for countless other nontraditional protests that evoked strong images of women. They affirmed that women have the "right, authority, and power to take control of the environment and the future . . . to dance and sing wherever we choose, . . . to bring color, life, and beauty to the deserts of concrete, electronics, and barbed wire made by men."[11]

## INDIVIDUALS FOR PEACEFUL CHANGE

Cherokee activist Wilma Mankiller understood how being poor and powerless led to violence. Many Native American communities were overwhelmed by alcohol abuse and domestic violence that stemmed from poor jobs, education, housing, and health of its members. In 1982, Mankiller challenged 300 Cherokee families from rural Bell, Oklahoma, to transform their lives, one step at a time. Together the community laid pipes for indoor plumbing. Then they built better homes. Within 14 months, hopelessness turned into pride as the people healed themselves. In 1987 the Cherokee Nation elected Mankiller as their first woman principal chief.[12]

Another powerful peace message came from Barbara Wiedner. Wiedner carried a sign that read "Grandmother for Peace" to her first protest against 150 nuclear weapons at the Mather Air Force Base in Sacramento, California. The following Good Friday she held the sign high as she blocked the base entrance and was arrested. "My Grandma loves us so much that she's gone to jail to save us from the bomb," was her grandson's reaction. Wiedner was moved by the faith children place in grandmothers. So she organized Grandmothers for Peace, now an international peace organization.[13]

Confidence from these protests captured the spirit of the United Nations Decade for Women. Fourteen thousand women from around the world attended the July 1985 United Nations Decade for Women: Equality, Development, and Peace conference in Nairobi, Kenya. The meeting signaled the close of the decade's activities but not the end of women's striving for a more peaceful world.

Listening to each other gave women from both industrialized and nonindustrialized nations a different outlook on peace. Activists from developing nations talked about experiences similar to Wilma Mankiller's. Military disarmament was still important. But the peace emphasis shifted toward changing the roots of everyday cruelty: hunger, unemployment, illiteracy, domestic violence, street crime, and torture of political prisoners.

One month later, demonstrators met in Washington, D.C., for the fortieth anniversary of the bombing of Hiroshima and Nagasaki. One hundred thousand people assembled for the Ribbon Project around the Pentagon. The ribbon was a vision of Justine Merrit, who began a banner in 1982 to remember loved ones lost to violence. Merrit pictured the ribbon as a symbol of peace encircling a symbol of war, the Pentagon.

Thousands of women from every state and across the oceans learned about the project by word of mouth. Women in prisons, convents, senior's groups, scout troops, and schools and from all walks of life embroidered, quilted, crocheted, and painted banners. State groups organized sew-ins and fund-raisers to cover transportation and mailing costs.

The August 4, 1985, mass demonstration signaled a new course of healing and renewal for women peace seekers. Demonstrators prayed for peace, marched to the Pentagon, and then assembled 10 miles of decorated ribbon panels around the Pentagon. Each panel represented about 25 hours of labor. Many artists had reproduced baby footprints, trees, children, and other life-affirming creations. A similar ribbon encircled the A-Bomb Memorial Dome in

Hiroshima. Local peace banners were displayed in parades, museums, and churches. Corvallis, Oregon, arranged a Ribbon Dance, and Allgau, Germany, held a Circle of Silence for Peace. Ribbon organizers described their project in a poem:

*We bring The Ribbon,*
*the work of thousands of hearts and hands,*
*to our nation's capital*
*as a gentle reminder*
*that we love the earth*
*and its peoples. . . .*
*This peace we seek*
*is much more than the absence of*
*war.*
*It is rather a peace that is rooted*
*in justice*
*and imbued with compassion. . . .*
*Together*
*we celebrate our human dignity*
*and own our vulnerability*
*in this nuclear age.*[14]

## THE BEGINNINGS OF ARMS CONTROL

On December 6, 1987, President Ronald Reagan and Soviet general secretary Mikhail Gorbachev signed the Intermediate-Range Nuclear Forces (INF) Treaty. The pact canceled an entire category of nuclear weapons. Equally important, the treaty became the first international attempt by superpowers to curb the arms race.

Over the next three years, Gorbachev initiated dramatic reforms in the Soviet Union, and with the election of Boris Yeltsin, the communist control of government ended. The Soviet Union broke apart into 15 countries, each struggling to maintain order, and the impact of the breakup echoed around the world. The surprised United States seemed pleased that the new Russia exerted less influence on its neighbors. By 1990, the Cold War ended.

Peace seekers seized the chance to lobby for scaled-down military budgets. Indeed, presidents George Bush and Bill Clinton cut army bases and recalled troops from NATO countries. But U.S. intelligence agents and military advisors remained in countless countries and backed terrorist governments that continually violated citizens' human rights.

In 1990, the U.S. military intervened when Iraq invaded neighboring Kuwait. The resulting Persian Gulf War reminded pacifists that full-scale war was only a bomb away. By 1995, the United States and former Soviet Union countries alone had 17,000 strategic nuclear weapons. Conservative U.S. legislators feared the nation's military advantage would diminish. They pressed to keep a strong military intact—just in case.

## NEIGHBORHOOD VIOLENCE

Modern peace builders had a different understanding of the changed military scene. Peace activist Ursula Franklin insisted, "If you want peace, work for justice. . . . [P]eace is not so much the absence of war as it is the absence of fear."[15]

Women peace activists continued to fight the old military mentality of fighting first and talking later. They viewed this philosophy as a primary reason why violence in the home and community increased so rapidly. Each year about 5,000 U.S. children died from violence. Thousands more died or suffered physical abuse from someone they knew.

Many neighborhoods were too dangerous for children to walk to school or play in playgrounds. Equally frightening was the news that children raised in violent environments often responded to conflict with violence. To ever achieve true peace, people must learn to treat each other better.

International networks of the WILPF, Women Strike for Peace, and scores of smaller organizations developed programs to break down barriers of race, religion, and gender that lead to misunderstanding. In the United States, women peace seekers battled the powerful gun lobby, television violence, and war toys for children.

Local educational programs reinforced the importance of resolving conflict through discussion and negotiation. Group leaders devised creative alternatives to lashing out when kids and adults get angry. Colleges from coast to coast held regular Take Back the Night marches to oppose violence against women.

In 1990, the Cape Cod Women's Agenda began the Clothesline Project National Network to put a human face on the shocking numbers of domestic abuse. Women strung clotheslines across the village green in Hyannis, Massachusetts. On the lines hung 31 color-coded shirts, each with the name of a domestic abuse sufferer. A gong rang every ten seconds, a whistle every three minutes, and a bell every fifteen minutes throughout the demonstration. Each sound reminded listeners of women who are beaten, raped, or killed with this frequency every day. By 1994, the network included more than 200 clotheslines and 20,000 T-shirts.

Women gained a major victory when President Clinton signed the Violence Against Women Act (1994) into law. Congress allocated funds for a national domestic violence hotline, battered women's shelters, and prosecution of offenders. Added money went to schools to devise programs that stifle sexual harassment before boys become battering young men.

In 1994, the Organization of American States approved a treaty that held 20 nations responsible for violence against women. The treaty offered a vehicle for individuals to file complaints if their government denied them protection against violence. This treaty was the first anywhere to recognize women's right to be free from violence.

One year later, however, only 7 of the 20 countries officially ratified the treaty. The United States buried the treaty in committee and has yet to sign. How strange that any government would refuse to sign anything that assured people human rights!

## COMMUNITY-BASED PROGRAMS

Such responses created another important aspect of women's peace work: self-help. Merely sending money, food, or supportive letters had little effect where widespread poverty and hopelessness existed. Former UN representative Mildred Robbin Leet saw firsthand how little money that a country received reached the poor. "So we came up with a process of directly reaching the people. . . . We saw starting a business as a way out of poverty."[16] In 1970, Leet founded Trickle Up, an international economic development organization. By 1995, the program had helped launch over 38,000 businesses that had served 250,000 people in more than 100 nations.

The 1992 Guatemalan Nobel Peace Prize winner Rigoberta Menchú believed in the community as a basis for change. She used her award money to fight for rights of native people everywhere. Menchú opened offices in Guatemala City, Mexico City, and New York to lobby international leaders for peaceful solutions to government cruelty.

In Guatemala, more than 150,000 people had been murdered or kidnapped by government soldiers, and 250,000 children had been orphaned. Menchú and supporters raised money for Guatemalan refugees who escaped government terror. Still, she continued to be a major player in negotiating peace between governments and Native American rebels seeking equal rights. She has made major inroads in organizing women to create ways to protect themselves.

The San Francisco Women's Building houses several grassroots programs for girls and women of color under one roof. Inside, the watchword is empowerment. Programs offer women the opportunity to lead peaceful and

productive lives. Bilingual services tackle domestic abuse, employment training, and refugee support. Outside the building is MaestraPeace, a colorful mural that illustrates women's unrecognized history, including a portrait of Rigoberta Menchú.

Women of color from every nation have intensified efforts to end harmful government practices. International groups based in the United States continue to monitor human rights worldwide. The Women's Rights Project of Human Rights Watch compiled reports on domestic violence in Brazil and Thailand. They discovered shocking accounts of Philippine and Chinese women forced into slavery to earn a living. Other sources revealed mail-order brides and families where girls are forbidden to go to school.

## UNITING FOR A PEACEFUL FUTURE

The 1995 United Nations Fourth World Conference on Women joined 5,000 delegates from 185 countries. Another 40,000 women attended nongovernment forums. The conference produced the strongest stands on human rights ever taken at a UN gathering. For the first time, a large public body agreed that women have a right to say no to sex without fear of violence. Further, women's right to nonviolent treatment was to override any national traditions, a bold step in many African and Asian countries.

The list of women's actions for peace is endless, and for good reason. The nuclear shadow and reality of violence and poverty are ever-present. As long as an underclass exists, uprisings threaten to burst into war. The story of conflict persisted in ancient days and through the U.S. Civil War and two world wars. Unfortunately, too much violence still poses great danger today.

Nonetheless, women peace seekers refuse to give up—not until harmony fills the planet. There will always be women willing to contribute to a peaceful world, each in her own way. Peace advocate and scientist Rosalie Bertell agrees:

*War-making needs to be relegated to the history books, along with castle-building, fortification of cities, dueling, cannibalism, and slavery. The nation's right to destroy its own people or those of other nations for some political advantages is as outrageous today as was the old custom establishing a male's right over the life of his spouse and children.[17]*

129

# WHAT YOU CAN DO TO PROMOTE PEACE                    11

*Never doubt that a small group of thoughtful committed citizens can change the world."[1]*

—Margaret Mead

**M**any women in this book took bold steps to achieve peace. They risked ridicule, jail, and in some instances their lives. In every case, they believed their cause of peace and justice was worth the danger. This faith in the power of what one person can do is what helps bring about change.

The world is getting smaller. Television, fax machines, and the Internet join inhabitants from the farthest corners of the world. Fallout from a nuclear accident in Russia affects the health of western Europeans. Government repression in Latin America sends thousands of refugees to the United States. Everyone is becoming more closely connected in ways never dreamed of years ago.

What you do with your life makes a difference—to your family and friends, your community, and the world. You may not resolve the world's problems alone. But you can touch the lives of those around you. By joining others who share your commitment, you can discover ways to solve urgent global problems. Women for peace join local groups or international organizations or extend a hand to their neighbor. You can too.

## PEACE BEGINS WITH YOU

Many of you want to do your part for peace but are unsure where to begin. Thinking about all the neglect, war, and suffering in the world can be overwhelming. Start by tackling one issue at a time. And the best place to begin is with what you know best—yourself.

### Consider your immediate world

The way you treat yourself and others provides some clues about whether you are a peaceful person. Everybody has bad days, but most people generally find pleasure in some aspects of their life. If you are unable to communicate needs and likes and dislikes without causing a fight, you may not feel too good inside. Similarly, if you are unable to set realistic goals, you may rarely achieve the successes that help you find pleasure in what you accomplish. What you think about yourself affects how you treat others.

If you are unhappy most of the time or find yourself continuously fighting, obtain help. Seek a trusted friend, parent, teacher, school counselor, or social worker. Allow someone to intervene on your behalf when you are unable to respond in ways other than fighting. Similarly, if your family handles disagreements with constant put-downs or physical abuse, tell a qualified outsider so you and your family can get help.

Peace builders make special efforts to treat people fairly. They resist violent solutions to conflict. They particularly oppose prejudice, greed, and taking advantage of those who are less able to defend themselves. Building a more peaceful world requires that you:

1. Understand the conflict in your own life and identify strategies to deal with these struggles. Keep a journal to

record your reactions to complex situations. Look for patterns in how you respond to friends and relatives. Decide if these patterns are productive. If not, think about creating alternatives to change how you handle conflict. Make sure you don't escape with drugs or alcohol, which can impair judgment. Ignore anyone who provokes a fight or tell an adult when another adult authority figure has unfair or harmful policies.

2. Accept another's point of view, even if you disagree. Let people know your views, too. Remember that the world would be a boring place if everyone thought and acted the same.

3. Practice being a good listener by looking at people when they talk. Genuinely pay attention. Ask questions to clarify what they say. Understand what feelings may lie beyond the words you hear.

4. Learn to solve problems together without anger. Work to resolve differences through discussion. Tell others your point of view without calling them names for disagreeing. Seek an objective person to help find solutions when you can't agree.

5. Be a peaceful role model for brothers, sisters, and friends.

### Consider your family, school, and larger community

One person can be a powerful force in motivating others toward a brighter, more just tomorrow. Learn as much as you can about what is going on in your community. Decide what issues interest you. Concentrate on one issue to improve your surroundings. Then discover creative ways to take action.

### CONFLICT RESOLUTION

Young people want to feel that what they say is heard, and most prefer to talk with other teens. You can become a peer advocate or mediator, someone who helps those in trouble settle disputes. If your school or neighborhood has no mediation program, suggest one. Ask a teacher, counselor, or community recreation worker to hold regular meetings where young people can come to resolve differences with an impartial board of peers. Request a bulletin board or special box where students can suggest conflict situations for discussion.

Emma Garcia started Teens on Target in Oakland, California, after a record-breaking year for local homicides. She and other teens were upset because so many friends died in one year. "Young people needed a place to talk about the deaths," Emma remembers.[2]

Teens on Target believes that young people care about what happens in their community. One reason teenagers often don't participate in programs is fear. Another is the lack of energy from so much else happening in their lives. Teens on Target trains young people as youth advocates to go into schools. Advocates talk with other young teens about the violence they face and ways to reduce it.

## LEARNING ANOTHER POINT OF VIEW

Better understanding and more peaceful interactions come from feeling comfortable with one another. Learn about other ethnic or disability groups represented in your school through reading or an interview. You can locate information at your school or neighborhood library or the Carter Center, founded by former president Jimmy Carter and his wife, Rosalynn Carter.

Volunteer to present background information to classmates about traditions and beliefs in your family. Ask teachers to include similar diverse ethnic ideas as part of class discussions. If you feel more should be done to integrate cultural knowledge in school, you can request that an elective course be offered to students.[3]

Teen peacemaker Detra Warfield proposed a black history course for Moore High School in Louisville, Kentucky.

from our permanent collection

🌿 AN EXHIBIT AT THE PEACE MUSEUM, LOCATED IN CHICAGO

She circulated a petition among students and throughout her community. The Jefferson County School Board liked the idea so much they created an African-American history elective course for the 10 high schools in the district.

Plan a trip for peace. Travel to the Chicago area and visit the Peace Museum. Marjorie Benton, former U.S. representative to UNICEF (United Nations International Children's Education Fund), founded the museum in 1981 to feature the "hidden history of peacemaking." Peace Museum programs and exhibits display art, writings, and musical materials. Traveling exhibits have shown heartfelt creations of artist Yoko Ono, peace folk singer Joan Baez, and survivors of the Hiroshima bombing. The museum is also home to segments of the Ribbon Project. You can volunteer at the museum, send donations to keep peaceful exhibits traveling, or write the museum for ideas to start your own peace museum.

You and your family may also enjoy national historic

sites that follow the Underground Railroad, the secret route to safety for runaway slaves, or Native American cultural centers. An especially important place to visit is the National Women's Hall of Fame in Seneca Falls, New York. Here you can view the place where the U.S. women's rights movements began and learn more exciting stories about famous female peacemakers.

## CELEBRATE PEACE

Too many national celebrations—Veteran's Day, Memorial Day, and in some communities a day for warriors, such as the Polish Revolutionary War general Kazimierz Pulaski— honor violence. Why not celebrate peace and those who promote justice instead?

Observe January 16 as Martin Luther King Jr. Day to learn about nonviolent protests and February as Black History Month to learn what African-Americans have accomplished.

Plan a program for International Women's Day on March 8. This date has been special for women factory workers since 1857. On that day, New York City women garment and textile workers protested low wages and a 12-hour workday. Three years later, in March 1860, the women formed a union to call for better working conditions and equal pay. On March 8, 1908, thousands of women garment workers marched for women's right to vote and an end to child labor.

Two years later, German labor leaders Clara Zetkin, Inessa Armand, and Nadezhda Krupskaya declared March 8 International Women's Day worldwide. The day was to "honor the historic struggle to improve women's lives." Eastern European countries observed the day regularly. It took the 1960s women's rights movement to highlight the day in the United States.

You can plan month-long events about women peacemakers in March, Women's History Month. In 1977, the Sonoma County, California, schools first decided to designate March as Women's History Month. Interest in including women in history led to the National Women's History Project in Santa Rosa, California, in 1980. The project became a national clearinghouse for materials about Women's Day and Women's History Month celebrations. In 1981, Congress proclaimed the week surrounding March 8 as Women's History Week.

Contact someone from local peace groups to talk at your school about peace issues. Ask representatives from these groups, Society of Friends, or antimilitary organizations to counter information from military recruiters. The military spends huge sums of money to attract teens to sign up for military service.

Organize a special planting project for Earth Day on April 22. Discover ways to preserve the world for the next generation. Suggest that your school present an award each month or year to students who have advanced peace and justice. Create your own special days, such as peace seeker Jane Addams's birthday on September 8.

Start a crane-folding program. Many young people fold paper cranes on August 6 to remember when the United States dropped the atomic bomb on Hiroshima in 1945. The activity was inspired by a true story described in the book *Sadako and the Thousand Paper Cranes* by Eleanor Coerr. According to Japanese tradition, anyone who folds 1,000 cranes has their wish come true. Young Sadako hoped to overcome radiation poisoning from the bomb by folding cranes. After completing 644 cranes, she died of leukemia. A memorial was established in her honor in the Hiroshima Peace Park in Hiroshima. Young people from around the world send cranes along with wishes for world peace to be placed at the memorial.

Hold peace celebrations that include an art exhibit displaying creative expressions for peace. Organize a sing-along that reflects the spirit of nonviolence, multicultural awareness, and a healthy environment. Make up your own songs about peace and nature. The programs can be fundraisers. Send the money you collect to a soup kitchen or homeless shelter.

IN 1947, A PEACE TREE WAS PLANTED AND A PEACE TOWER UNVEILED TO COMMEMORATE THE SECOND ANIVERSARY OF THE DROPPING OF AN ATOMIC BOMB ON HIROSHIMA.

Many peace groups publish newsletters or other information to distribute free or for the cost of mailing. Display the material, perhaps on a special "Teens for Peace" bulletin board. Ask your public and school libraries to subscribe to peace publications. Borrow, rent, or purchase videos that discuss peace and social justice issues that interest you. Hold a video party concerning the topic or ask your teacher to show the movie in class.

Some peace groups are communicating on the Internet. Peacenet is the most active e-mail source. Join other peace surfers around the world in celebrating a more just world.

## WEAPONS CONTROL

Each year, more young people die from guns than from cancer, AIDS, and heart disease combined.[4] And the numbers keep rising. Push for a weapon-free home and school. Start a newsletter that lets your peers know how handguns hurt lives of victims and those who know the victim.

If your parents keep a firearm, explain that a gun in the home actually increases the chance that a loved one will be killed or injured or will succeed in committing suicide. Help parents understand that a gun in the house is 43 times more likely to kill a family member or friend than provide self-defense.[5]

Urge friends and relatives who keep a handgun to turn it in to a police department that melts down firearms. If gun keepers refuse to remove the weapon from their home, encourage them to store unloaded firearms and ammunition in separate locked locations.

Persuade your parents to remove war toys younger brothers and sisters may have. Gather information about gun control that young children can understand. Organize a group to go into classes of younger students to talk about the dangers of guns. Make posters for your school, community center, and neighborhood that show these are gun-free zones. Collect letters or signatures on a petition that endorses banning guns. Send them to local, state, and federal government representatives.

## SUBSTANCE ABUSE

Alcohol and drug abuse endangers the lives of users as well as those who suffer from their frightening behavior. Cigarettes threaten the health of smokers and those around them. Contact your local town hall or police department to protest liquor and cigarette stores and advertisements located too near schools and playgrounds. Spend your money at stores that uphold laws that limit the sale of these goods to minors.

## ENVIRONMENT

A Kenyan proverb says, "We have not inherited this earth from our parents, rather it was loaned to us by our children."[6] Use the land and energy wisely. Help your family recycle paper, plastic, and aluminum goods. Offer to separate recycling waste for a neighbor who is unable to carry garbage. Make sure your school and community has recycling. If not, help them start a program.

You can also pick up litter in school and from streets, beaches, parks, and highways. Organize family members or a group of friends to help you on a regular basis. As you work, wear a button or T-shirt emblazoned with a message for peace, justice, or the environment.

Conserve water and electricity. Turn off faucets and lights when not in use. Just turning off the water after you wet your toothbrush and before you rinse your mouth saves gallons of water each day.

Encourage your parents to plant more shrubs and trees outside. Start a planting club in your neighborhood. If there are empty lots, ask the owner if you and some friends can plant a vegetable or flower garden.

Joshua Elliott helped found the Hamilton, New York, Teen Peacemakers. Although Josh died in 1991, his efforts led to teen programs that maintained bluebird houses at an environmental center. Teen Peacemakers also planted 1,200 evergreen seedlings in the Oneida Native American Territory.[7]

## PEACE CAMPS

In 1983, a 12-year-old girl from Auburn, Maine, feared nuclear war between the United States and Soviet Union.

SAMANTHA SMITH LOOKS OVER A BULGARIAN NEWSPAPER
THAT CONTAINS A STORY OF HER UPCOMING VISIT TO THE
SOVIET UNION. IN 1983, THE 12-YEAR-OLD WAS INVITED
TO VISIT THE SOVIET UNION TO SEE THAT SOVIET
CHILDREN ALSO WANTED TO END THE THREAT OF WAR.

Samantha Smith wrote a letter about her deep concerns to
Soviet leader Yuri Andropov. In the letter she asked, "Why
do you want to conquer the whole world, or at least our
country?" Andropov returned Samantha's letter with an invitation to visit children in the Soviet Union. That way, she
could see that children everywhere, even in the Soviet
Union, wanted an end to the threat of war.

Samantha had a much-publicized trip that gained her fame as a peacemaker. But she and her father died in a plane crash the following year. Her mother created the Samantha Smith Center in her memory, and Maine proclaimed the first Monday in June as Samantha Smith Day. The Samantha Smith Center publishes a newsletter about peace and raises money to send youngsters on peacekeeping missions worldwide through Worldpeace Camp.

Since Samantha's visit, several peace camps have opened to send teenagers to foreign countries. Other agencies bring teens to the United States. You can travel to a peace camp in another country or invite a foreign camper to your home. Travelers share common and not-so-common experiences with other teens. They build peaceful bridges between nations, just like Samantha began with teens in the Soviet Union.

International Peace Games, a local peace-building program in Boston, Massachusetts, sends college and community volunteers into elementary-school classrooms. Volunteers create cooperative projects similar to peace camp experiences. After 18 weeks, the students are joined by international students on a 10-day visit.

You can also volunteer to work with people from poorer countries. Spend a summer or school year overseas helping in an orphanage or community service center. If you like to be outdoors, volunteer to help plant a garden or build a hospital.

## LEND A HELPING HAND

A good way to foster peace is to help reduce the hardships of poverty. Volunteer or recruit volunteers to work in soup kitchens or homeless shelters. Enlist friends for a food, clothing, or toy drive. Spend a week or two with a group like Habitat for Humanity, building homes for homeless families.

Some hotlines train teens to talk with teens. You could assist someone who has trouble with schoolwork. Or you could help runaways, depressed youth, or victims of rape and abuse.

If you live in the city, locate a Big Sister or Big Brother project. There are also Special Olympics or Best Buddies nationwide where you can spend time with someone who has a disability. With Big Sisters or Best Buddies, you need to commit to regular visits with your new friend. You can tutor, go places, or provide an understanding ear. Ask a teacher, social worker, or religious leader to organize a partner program, if none exists.

## MONITOR HUMAN RIGHTS ABUSES

Each year millions of children die and others barely escape death from harsh governments. Millions more live in poverty, including many in the United States. Throughout the world, thousands of men, women, and children are tortured and imprisoned for their beliefs. Many receive no trials. They merely disappear, never to be seen again.

If you want to help, join national and international welfare organizations that monitor human rights. You may want to start a school group such as an Amnesty International branch. These groups provide information about individuals who need your support. You can send petitions or letters to government leaders on their behalf or raise money for their families.

## MEDIA WATCH

Did you know that by the time the average young person in the United States reaches sixth grade, he or she will have seen 8,000 murders on television? That means watching about two killings per day. Action-packed television shows give young people the message that violence is not only commonplace but acceptable. Many depict women as victims of violence and minorities in stereotype roles that are demeaning.

Boycott violent television shows and movies or those

biased against women and minorities. If you happen to view a show that is antipeace, write a protest letter to the station. You can also write to sponsors through their customer relations department. Let them know you refuse to buy products from a company that supports shows that are violent or degrade one segment of the population.

Write, petition, protest, speak out, march, reach out—anything to get involved. Let peace begin with you!

# SOURCE NOTES

**Chapter One**

1. Quoted in Sara Ruddick, *Maternal Thinking: Toward a Politics of Peace* (Boston: Beacon Press, 1989), p. 151.
2. Milton Meltzer, *Ain't Gonna Study War No More* (New York: Harper & Row, 1985), p. 10.
3. Jimmy Carter, *Talking Peace* (New York: Dutton, 1993), p. 58.
4. Lauren Tarshis, "Waging Peace," *Scholastic Update* 123 (Feb. 8, 1991), p. 18.
5. Ibid., p. 4.
6. Carter, p. 58.
7. Jean Bethke Elshtain, *Women and War* (New York: Basic Books, 1987), p. 97.
8. Ibid., p. 99.
9. Natalie Angier, "Does Testosterone Equal Aggression? Maybe Not," *New York Times*, June 20, 1995, p. 1.
10. Judith Porter Adams, *Peacework: Oral Histories of Women Peace Activists* (Boston: Twayne, 1990), p. 188.
11. Quoted in Ursula Franklin, "Women and Militarism,"

*Canadian Woman Studies*, v. 9, no. 1, pp. 5–6, and paraphrased in Adrienne Harris, *Rocking the Ship of State* (San Francisco: Westview Press, 1989), p. 134.
12. Tarshis, pp. 11–12.

## Chapter Two
1. C. A. Robinson, ed., *Lysistrata, An Anthology of Greek Drama* (New York: Rinehart, 1953), p. 245.
2. From *The Holy Bible: New Revised Standard Version* (Nashville: Thomas Nelson, 1989), 1 Samuel 28.11.
3. Berenice Carroll, " 'Women take action!': Women's Direct Action and Social Change," *Women's Studies International Forum*, v. 12, no. 1, 1989, p.3.
4. Gloria Steinem, *Revolution from Within* (New York: Little, Brown, 1993), p. 312.
5. Mitchell Carroll, *Woman in All Ages and in All Countries* (Philadelphia: Rittenhouse, 1908), p. 260.
6. B. Carroll, p. 5.
7. Meltzer, p. 13.
8. Quoted in Jean Bethke Elshtain, *Women and War* (New York: Basic Books, 1987), pp. 132–33.
9. B. Carroll, p. 5.
10. Eleanor Flexner, *Century of Struggle* (Cambridge, MA: Belknap Press, 1975), pp. 7–8.

## Chapter Three
1. Quoted in Harriet Hyman Alonso, *Peace as a Women's Issue* (Syracuse, NY: Syracuse University Press, 1993), p. 38.
2. Quoted in Joseph Bruchac, *Stone Giants and Flying Heads* (Trumansburg, NY: Crossing Press, 1979), p. 25.
3. Doreen Rappaport, *American Women: Their Lives in Their Words* (New York: Crowell, 1990), p. 40.
4. Quoted in Helen Michalowski, ed., *Power of the People* (San Francisco: Peace Press, 1977), p. 15.
5. Michalowski, p. 16.
6. Quoted in Flexner, p. 13.

7. Quoted in Flexner, p. 15.
8. Quoted in Alonso, p. 26.
9. Quoted in Emily Taft Douglas, *Remember the Ladies* (New York: Putnam, 1966), pp. 72–73.
10. Quoted in Flexner, p. 45.

**Chapter Four**
1. Alonso, p. 36.
2. Ibid.
3. Ibid., p. 27.
4. Quoted in Grace Humphrey, *Women in American History* (New York: Bobbs-Merrill, 1919), p. 123.
5. B. Carroll, p. 12.
6. Quoted in B. Carroll, p. 9.
7. Elizabeth Frost, *Women's Suffrage in America* (New York: Facts on File, 1992), p. 28.
8. Quoted in Alonso, pp. 32–33.
9. Quoted in Rappaport, pp. 61–62.
10. Quoted in Alonso, pp. 42–43.
11. Quoted in Alonso, p. 44.
12. Ibid.

**Chapter Five**
1. Quoted in Harriet Sigerman, *Laborers for Liberty* (New York: Oxford University Press, 1994), p. 134.
2. Amy Swerdlow, *Women Strike for Peace* (Chicago: University of Chicago Press, 1993), p. 27.
3. Flexner, p. 182.
4. B. Carroll, p.16.
5. Patrick Reardon, "The Memphis Years of Ida B. Wells," *Chicago Tribune*, January 22, 1995.
6. Joy James, "The Anti-Violence Legacy of an Ancestor Mother: Ida B. Wells-Barnett," *Community Times*, vol. 2, no. 2 (Feb. 1995), p. 1.
7. Ibid., p. 8.
8. Swerdlow, p. 29.
9. Alonso, p. 49.

## Chapter Six

1. Quoted in Elshtain, p. 145.
2. Alonso, pp. 52–54.
3. Alonso, p. 54.
4. Catherine Foster, *Women for All Seasons* (Athens: University of Georgia Press, 1989), p. 14.
5. Swerdlow, p. 30
6. Ibid.
7. Quoted in Swerdlow, p. 30.
8. Quoted in Swerdlow, p. 31.
9. Quoted in Foster, p. 15.
10. Charles Chatfield, *For Peace and Justice* (Boston: Beacon Press, 1971), pp. 18–19.
11. Alonso, p. 70.
12. Chatfield, p. 22.
13. Quoted in Swerdlow, p. 32
14. Quoted in Alonso, p. 13.
15. Alonso, p. 83.

## Chapter Seven

1. Quoted in Michalowski, p. 83.
2. Alonso, p. 85.
3. Quoted in Alonso, p. 87.
4. Mary Gray Peck, *Carrie Chapman Catt: A Biography* (New York: Wilson, 1944), p. 370.
5. Leaflet from the No More War Parade Committee, 1935. Swarthmore College Peace Collection.
6. Quoted in Nancy Cott, *The Grounding of Modern Feminism* (New Haven, CT: Yale University Press, 1987), p. 246.
7. Quoted in Alonso, p. 111.
8. Quoted in Swerdlow, p. 34.
9. Swerdlow, p.35; Michalowski, p. 43.
10. Paula Giddings, *When and Where I Enter: The Impact of Black Women on Race and Sex in America* (New York: Bantam, 1984), pp. 232–33.

## Chapter Eight

1. Rita Mae Brown, *High Hearts* (New York: Bantam Books, 1986), p. 413.
2. Michalowski, p. 81.
3. Quoted in Michalowski, p. 79.
4. Quoted in Alonso, p. 138.
5. Interview quoted in Foster, pp. 22–23.
6. Elaine Tyler May, *Pushing the Limits: American Women 1940–1961* (New York: Oxford University Press, 1994), pp. 23–29.
7. B. Carroll, p. 14.
8. May, p. 63.
9. Quoted in May, p. 31.
10. Quoted in Alonso, p. 162.
11. Quoted in Alonso, p. 165.
12. Quoted in Alonso, p. 186.

## Chapter Nine

1. Quoted in Amnesty International, *Of Human Rights: Giving Form to a Dream*, p. 1.
2. May, p. 54.
3. Swerdlow, p. 43.
4. Quoted in May, p. 132.
5. U.S. Congressional Committee Hearing, (86) S1337-1, p. 274.
6. U.S. Congressional Committee Hearing, (87) H1966-2, p. 2200.
7. Ibid.
8. Melba Pattillo Beals, *Warriors Don't Cry* (New York: Simon & Schuster, 1994), p. 1.
9. Quoted in Swerdlow, p. 91.
10. Pam Allister, "Songs for Peace and Freedom," *Women of Power*, 10 (Summer 1998), p. 8.
11. Interview with Pearl Hirshfield, March 1995.
12. Quoted in Alonso, pp. 222–23.
13. Swerdlow, p. xi.
14. Quoted in May, p. 125.
15. Rappaport, p. 253.

16. Quoted in Alonso, p. 218.
17. Quoted in *Give Peace a Chance* (Chicago: Chicago Review Press, 1983) p. 11.

## Chapter 10
1. Adams, p. 190.
2. Alonso, pp. 243–44.
3. Franklin, p. 20.
4. Quoted in Alonso, p. 229.
5. Quoted in Alonso, p. 243.
6. Quoted in *Current Biography*, 1983, p. 42.
7. Alonso, p. 245.
8. Quoted in Adrienne Harris, *Rocking the Ship of State* (Boulder, CO: Westview Press, 1989), p. 287.
9. Barrie Newman, "Peace Movement Imagery," *Society* (March/April, 1986), p. 28.
10. Alonso, p. 255.
11. B. Carroll, p. 17.
12. Gloria Steinem, "A New Kind of Leader," *Ms.* (Nov/Dec, 1991), p. 29.
13. Sally Roesch Wagner, "Global Grandmother," *Woman of Power*, Issue Ten, p. 37.
14. Marianne Philbin, ed., *The Ribbon: A Celebration of Life* (Asheville, NC: Lark, 1987), p. 26.
15. Franklin, p. 21.
16. Linda Lehrer, "Trickle Up," *Chicago Tribune*, October 23, 1994.
17. Rosalie Bertell, "Early War Crimes of WWIII," *Canadian Women Studies*, vol. 9, no. 1, p. 6.

## Chapter 11
1. Quoted in Women for Peace brochure, 1995.
2. Interview with Emma Garcia, Teens On Target, April 7, 1995.
3. Detra Warfield, "Teen Adds to History," *Peace on Our Minds* (Winter 1991), p. 10.
4. A. L. Kellerman and D. T. Reay, "Protection or Peril? An Analysis of Firearms-related Deaths in the Home,"

*New England Journal of Medicine*, (314:1557–60); re-searched by Laurie Duker, "Firearms Facts" distributed by the Children's Safety Network at the National Center for Education in Maternal and Child Health.

5. Mark Bregman, "Teens and a Killer Disease," *Science World* (vol. 51, no. 3, Oct. 7, 1994), p. 7.

6. Quoted in Alonso, p. 258.

7. Hamilton Teen Peacemakers, "Peacemaker Joshua Elliott, 13, Stood for Life, Justice and a Green and Healthy World," *Peace on Our Minds* (Spring 1991), p. 15.

# For Further Information

1

## BOOKS

Aaseng, Nathan. *The Peace Seekers*. Minneapolis: Lerner, 1987.

Adams, Judith Porter. *Peacework: Oral Histories of Women Peace Activists*. Boston: Twayne, 1990.

Alonso, Harriet Hyman. *Peace as a Women's Issue: History of the United States Movement for World Peace and Women's Rights*. Syracuse, NY: Syracuse University Press, 1993.

Beals, Melba Pattillo. *Warriors Don't Cry*. New York: Simon & Schuster, 1994.

Bentley, Judith. *The Nuclear Freeze Movement*. New York: Franklin Watts, 1984.

Carter, Jimmy. *Talking Peace*. New York: Dutton, 1993.

Flexner, Eleanor. *Century of Struggle*. Cambridge, MA: Belknap Press, 1975.

Humphrey, Grace. *Women in American History*. New York: Bobbs-Merrill, 1919.

Kronenwetter, Michael. *The Peace Commandos*. New York: New Discovery, 1994.

Mayers, Teena Karsa. *Understanding Nuclear Weapons and Arms Control*, 3rd ed. Washington: Pergammon-Brassey's, 1986.

Meltzer, Milton. *Ain't Gonna Study War No More*. New York: Harper & Row, 1985.

Near, Holly. *The Great Peace March*. New York: Holt & Company, 1993

Opfell, Olga. *The Lady Laureates: Women Who Have Won the Nobel Peace Prize*. 2nd ed. Metuchen, NJ: Scarecrow, 1986.

Rappaport, Doreen. *American Women: Their Lives in Their Words*. New York: Crowell, 1990.

Sigerman, Harriet. *Laborers for Liberty: American Women 1865–1890*. New York: Oxford University Press, 1994.

Webster-Doyle, Terrence. *Why Is Everybody Always Picking on Me: A Guide to Handling Bullies*. Middlebury, VT: Atrium Society, 1991.

## Articles

Carroll, Berenice. " 'Women take action!': Women's Direct Action and Social Change." *Women's Studies International Forum* vol. 12, no. 1, (1989), pp. 1–13.

*Ms.* "The Many Faces of Feminism." (July/August 1994): 33–63.

Reardon, Patrick. "The Memphis Years of Ida B. Wells." *Chicago Tribune* (Jan. 22, 1995): 7.

Sherrid, Pamela. "Peaceniks Packing Up." *U.S. News and World Report* (Dec. 7, 1987).

Tannehauser, Carol. "Passion with a Purpose, Women with a Cause." *Woman's Day* (Jan. 20, 1987): 147–48.

Tarshis, Lauren. "Waging Peace." *Scholastic Update* 123 (Feb. 8, 1991): 4–20.

## INTERNET SITES

Because of the changeable nature of the internet, sites appear and disappear very quickly. These resources offered useful information on peace at the time of publication. Internet addresses must be entered with capital and lowercase letters exactly as they appear.

IANWeb Resources-Peace and Conflict Resolution
**http://www.pitt.edu/~ian/Resources/iat-peac.html**

Peace Planet
**http://www.teleport.com/~amt/peaceplanet/index.shtml**

Peace Memorial Museum
**http://www.csi.adijp:8081/ABOMB/pmm.html**

Children's Peace Memorial
**http://www.fyisoft.com/~emc2/**

Peace Discussion Group
**listprof@csf.colorado.edu**

# Appendix

## Organizations You Can Contact for a Better World

*How do you feel at the end of the day in a peaceful world? Take a few deep breaths and prepare to awaken. Bring with you this peaceful world. When you are ready, open your eyes. Awaken in Peace!*

—Adapted from *The Inner Dance* by Diane Mariechild

American Friends Service
  Committee
Material Aid Division
1515 Cherry Street
Philadelphia, Pennsylvania 19102

Amnesty International
322 Eighth Avenue
10th Floor
New York, New York 10001
212/807-8400

Best Buddies
1350 New York Avenue NW
Washington, D.C. 20005
202/347-7265

Carter Center
Jimmy Carter Library and
  Museum
1 Copenhill Avenue
Atlanta, Georgia 30307
404/420-5100

Habitat for Humanity—Midwest
  Region
1920 South Laflin
Chicago, Illinois
312/243-6448

Human Rights Watch
Women's Rights Project
485 Fifth Avenue
New York, New York 10017

Illinois Council for the Prevention
  of Violence
220 South State Street
Suite 1215
Chicago, Illinois 60604

International Peace Games
Harvard University
Phillips Brooks House
  Association
Cambridge, Massachusetts
  02138-6533

Madre
121 West 27th Street, Room 301
New York, New York 10001

Mennonite Peace Center
528 East Madison
Lombard, Illinois 60148

National Peace Foundation
Transcaucasus Women's Dialogue
1835 K Street NW
Suite 610
Washington, D.C. 20006
202/223-1770

National Women's Hall of Fame
76 Fall Street
P.O. Box 335
Seneca Falls, New York 13148
315/568-8060

National Women's History
  Project
7738 Bell Road
Windsor, California 95492
707/838-6000

Network of East-West Women
395 Riverside Drive
Suite 2F
New York, New York 10025
212/749-6798

Peace Action
1819 H Street, NW
Suite 640
Washington, D.C. 20006-3603

Peace Links
729 Eighth Street, SE
Suite 300
Washington, DC 20003

The Peace Museum
350 West Ontario
4th Floor
Chicago, Illinois 60610
312/440-1860

Peace Park
Hiroshima Peace Memorial
  Museum
1-3 Nagajima-cho
Hiroshima, 733 Japan

Promoting Enduring Peace
P.O. Box 5103
Woodmont, CT 06460
203/878-4769

Samantha Smith Center
9 Union Street
Hallowell, Maine 04347
207/626-3415

Special Olympics International
Suite 500
1350 New York Avenue, NW
Washington, D.C. 20005
202/628-3630

Teens on Target/Youth Alive
3012 Summit Avenue
Suite 3670
Summit Medical Center
Oakland, California 94609
510/444-6191

United States Committee for
  UNICEF
331 East 38th Street
New York, New York 10016
212/686-5522

Volunteers for Peace International
  World Camps
43 Tiffany Road
Belmont, Vermont 05730
802/259-2759

Women Strike for Peace
110 Maryland Avenue, NE
Suite 302
Washington, D.C. 20002
202/543-2660

Women for Women in Bosnia
P.O. Box 9733
Alexandria, Virginia 22304
703/519-1730

Women's Building/Edificio de
  Mujeres
San Francisco Women's Centers,
  Inc.
3543 18th Street, #8
San Francisco, California 94110
415/431-1180

Women's International League for
  Peace and Freedom
1213 Race Street
Philadelphia, Pennsylvania
  19107-1691
215/563-7110

WorldPeace Camp
c/o Samantha Smith Center
9 Union Street
Hallowell, Maine 04347
207/626-3415
(They publish *Peace Camp
Handbook and Curriculum
Guide.*)

Media Contacts
Women Make Movies
225 Lafayette Street
Suite 212
New York, New York 10012

The Educational Film and Video
  Project
1529 Josephine Street
Berkeley, California 94703

# Index